The Wisdom of the East Series
东方智慧丛书
Editors-in-Chief: Tang Wenhui   Liu Zhiqiang
主编：汤文辉   刘志强
Academic Adviser: Zhang Baoquan
学术顾问：张葆全

Chinese-English
汉 英 对 照

Three-Character Classic

三 字 经

Written by（Song Dynasty）Wang Yinglin
原著：（宋）王应麟
Commented by Wang Zhuan
释析：王专
Proofread by Zhang Baoquan
中文审读：张葆全
Translated by Shen Fei
翻译：沈菲
Illustrated by Wang Xuefeng   Tao Chaolai   Lü Peng
绘图：王雪峰   陶朝来   吕鹏

· 桂林 Gui Lin ·

GUANGXI NORMAL UNIVERSITY PRESS
广西师范大学出版社

图书在版编目（CIP）数据

三字经：汉英对照 / 王专释析；沈菲译；王雪峰，
陶朝来，吕鹏绘. —桂林：广西师范大学出版社，
2016.9（2017.5 重印）
（东方智慧丛书 / 汤文辉等主编）
ISBN 978-7-5495-8533-5

Ⅰ. ①三… Ⅱ. ①王…②沈…③王…④陶…⑤吕…
Ⅲ. ①古汉语－启蒙读物－汉、英 Ⅳ. ①H194.1

中国版本图书馆 CIP 数据核字（2016）第 167914 号

广西师范大学出版社出版发行

（广西桂林市中华路 22 号　邮政编码：541001）
网址：http://www.bbtpress.com
出版人：张艺兵
全国新华书店经销
桂林广大印务有限责任公司印刷
（桂林市临桂县秧塘工业园西城大道北侧广西师范大学出版社集团
有限公司创意产业园　邮政编码：541100）
开本：880 mm × 1 240 mm　1/32
印张：9.375　字数：164 千字　图：87 幅
2016 年 9 月第 1 版　2017 年 5 月第 2 次印刷
定价：76.00 元

如发现印装质量问题，影响阅读，请与印刷厂联系调换。

总　序

　　文化交流对人类社会的存在与发展至关重要。季羡林先生曾指出，文化交流是推动人类社会前进的主要动力之一，文化一旦产生，就必然交流，这种交流是任何力量也阻挡不住的。由于文化交流，世界各民族的文化才能互相补充，共同发展，才能形成今天世界上万紫千红的文化繁荣现象。[1]

　　中国与东盟国家的文化交流亦然，并且具有得天独厚的优势。首先，中国与东盟许多国家地理相接，山水相连，不少民族之间普遍存在着跨居、通婚现象，这为文化交流奠定了良好的地理与人文基础。其次，古代中国与世界其他国家建立起的"海上丝绸之路"为中国与东盟国家的经济、文化交流创造了有利的交通条件。

　　中国与东盟诸多使用不同语言文字的民族进行思想与文化对话，

---

[1]季羡林：《文化的冲突与融合·序》，载张岱年、汤一介等《文化的冲突与融合》，北京大学出版社，1997年，第2页。

自然离不开翻译。翻译活动一般又分为口译和笔译两类。有史记载的中国与东盟之间的口译活动可以追溯至西周时期，但笔译活动则出现在明代，至今已逾五百年的历史。

在过去五百年的历史长河中，东盟国家大量地译介了中国的文化作品，其中不少已经融入到本国的文化中去。中国译介东盟国家的作品也不在少数。以文字为载体的相互译介活动，更利于文化的传承与发展，把中国与东盟国家的文化交流推上了更高的层次。

2013 年 9 月，国务院总理李克强在广西南宁举行的第十届中国—东盟博览会开幕式上发表主旨演讲时指出，中国与东盟携手开创了合作的"黄金十年"。他呼吁中国与东盟百尺竿头更进一步，创造新的"钻石十年"。2013 年 10 月，习近平总书记在周边外交工作座谈会上强调要对外介绍好我国的内外方针政策，讲好中国故事，传播好中国声音，把中国梦同周边各国人民过上美好生活的愿望、同地区发展前景对接起来，让命运共同体意识在周边国家落地生根。于是，把中华文化的经典译介至东盟国家，不仅具有重要的历史意义，同时还蕴含着浓厚的时代气息。

所谓交流，自然包括"迎来送往"，《礼记》有言："往而不来，非礼也；来而不往，亦非礼也。"中国与东盟国家一样，既翻译和引进外国的优秀文化，同时也把本国文化的精髓部分推介出去。作为中国最具人文思想的出版社之一——广西师范大学出版社构想了《东方智慧丛书》，并付诸实践，不仅是中国翻译学界、人文学界的大事，更是中国与东盟进行良好沟通、增进相互了解的必然选择。广东外语外贸大学和广西民族大学作为翻译工作的主要承担方，都是国家外语非通用语种本科人才培养基地，拥有东盟语言文字的翻译优势。三个单位的合作将能够擦出更多的火花，向东盟国家更好地传播中华文化。

联合国教科文组织的官员认为，"文化交流是新的全球化现象"。[1]
我们希望顺应这一历史潮流与时代趋势，做一点力所能及的事。

是为序。

刘志强

2015 年 1 月 25 日

---

[1]《联合国教科文组织文化政策与跨文化对话司司长卡特瑞娜·斯泰诺的致辞》，载《世界文化的东亚视角》，北京大学出版社，2004年，第3页。

Preface to The Wisdom of the East Series

Cultural exchanges are of significant importance to the existence and development of human society. Mr. Ji Xianlin once pointed out that cultural exchange was one of the major driving forces for the progress of human society. It is inevitable that communications and exchanges will occur among different cultures. As a result, the interaction and mutual enrichment of cultures contribute to the formation of a diversified world featured by cultural prosperity.[1]

The cultural exchange between China and ASEAN countries, in the trend of mutual communication and interaction, also boasts of its own unique strengths. First of all, China borders many ASEAN countries both by land and by sea, and intermarriage and transnational settlement are common, all of which lay a solid foundation for cultural exchanges. In addition, the "Maritime Silk

---

[1] Ji Xianlin, "Preface to Cultural Conflicts and Integration", in *Cultural Conflicts and Integration*, edited by Zhang Dainian, Tang Yijie, et al. Beijing: Beijing University Press, 1997, p.2.

Road" developed by ancient China and other countries has helped pave the way to a smooth economic and cultural exchange between China and ASEAN countries.

People from China and ASEAN countries use different languages. Thus, to conduct a successful dialogue in the cultural field requires the involvement of translation and oral interpretation. Historical records show that the oral interpretation among people of China and ASEAN can be dated back to the Western Zhou Dynasty (1122-771 B.C.). It is also known that translation started to boom in the Ming Dynasty, which was five hundred years ago.

In the past five hundred years, a large number of Chinese cultural works were translated into many languages of ASEAN countries and many of which have been integrated into their local cultures. China has also translated a lot of works of ASEAN countries. Translation is beneficial to inheritance and development of culture and upgrades the cultural exchanges between China and ASEAN to a higher level.

As Mr. Li Keqiang, Premier of the State Council of the People's Republic of China, pointed out in his speech at the opening ceremony of the 10th China-ASEAN Expo held in Nanning in September, 2013, China and ASEAN jointly created "10 golden years" of cooperation. And he called on both sides to upgrade their cooperation to a new level by creating "10 diamond years". In October, 2013, General Secretary Xi Jinping emphasized, in a meeting with Chinese diplomats, the importance of introducing China's domestic and foreign policies to other countries and regions, and making Chinese voice heard in the world. Xi also pointed out that "Chinese Dream" should be connected with her neighboring countries' dream of a better life and with the development prospect of those countries so as to build up a community of shared destiny. Against such a backdrop, it's of both historical and current significance to translate Chinese classics and introduce them to ASEAN countries.

Exchanges are reciprocal. According to *The Book of Rites*, behaviors that do not reciprocate are not consistent with rites. Like ASEAN countries, China has had excellent foreign cultural works translated and introduced domestically, and also translate and introduce to the outside world the essence of local culture and thoughts. Guangxi Normal University Press, one of the top presses in China that focus on enhancing the influence of the humanities, made the decision to publish *The Wisdom of the East Series*. It is not only a big event in Chinese academia, but also a necessary choice for China and ASEAN to communicate with each other and enhance mutual understanding. Guangdong University of Foreign Studies, and Guangxi University for Nationalities, the main undertakers of the translation project, are both national non-universal languages training bases for undergraduates and boast strengths of ASEAN languages. Cooperation between the two universities and the press will surely facilitate dissemination of traditional Chinese culture to ASEAN countries.

UNESCO officials hold the belief that cultural exchange is a new phenomenon of globalization.[1] We hope that our efforts could breathe the spirit of this historical momentum and help ASEAN countries understand Chinese culture better.

Liu Zhiqiang

January 25, 2015

---

[1] "Speech of Katerina stenou, Director of Division of Cultural Policies and Intercultural Dialogue", from *East Asia's View on World Culture*. Beijing: Beijing University Press, 2004, p.3.

三字经
Three-Character Classic

前　言

《三字经》是中国家喻户晓的儿童启蒙教育经典。

《三字经》的编著者，一般认为是南宋学者王应麟。在王应麟编定《三字经》以后，明、清以至民国学者屡次增补，主要是增加了宋至清末的王朝变迁内容。

《三字经》全文虽仅 1134 字，内容却丰富广博，包含了中国古代的教育和学习的方法、伦理道德以及天文地理、诸子百家、历代兴衰等基本常识。为使全文层次清晰、便于阅读和记诵，可根据文意，将《三字经》按顺序分为"首重孝悌""增广见闻""通读经子""熟读诸史""勉力勤学"五个部分。

学童在"首重孝悌"部分可以了解儒家最基本、最核心的礼教规范和伦理道德，这些礼教规范和伦理道德是中国古代道德文明的基石，是德育培养的根本。

在"增广见闻"部分从认识数目开始，延伸到日常生活，了解并掌握生活所需的基本常识。

在"通读经子"部分可以知道中国传统文化必读的经典书目及读这些经典的先后顺序，可以了解中国丰富的经典文献和绚丽灿烂的中华文化，进而热爱中国传统文化。

在"熟读诸史"部分不仅可以了解中国历代兴亡，还可以了解其兴衰成败的原因，并可以逐步认识到中国大一统和多民族融合的历史趋势。

在"勉力勤学"部分可以通过历史上勤勉好学的范例，以及历史人物的嘉言懿行受到激励，并以之为榜样，奋发勤学、显亲扬名。

《三字经》如此丰富的内容，蕴含着系统的教育思想。它以儒家思想为核心，主张孝悌为本、立德为要，进而教育学童通四书、晓五经、阅诸子、明历史。它十分强调持之以恒与知行合一的重要性，劝勉学童志存高远、奋发图强，最终成为德才兼备之人。

形式上，《三字经》采用了三言韵语，三字一句，短小精悍，读起来朗朗上口；同时，前后连贯，衔接自然，段与段之间不仅有内容上的关联，还用数字进行了连接，从三才、三纲到四时、四方；从五行、五常到六谷、六畜；从七情、八音，最后到九族、十义，过渡自然巧妙，十分方便学童记诵。

"熟读《三字经》，可知千古事"，从它一问世，就被赞为"袖里通鉴纲目"，因而流传广泛，历代都被奉为经典。《三字经》独特的思想内容和形式结构至今仍具有价值和魅力，值得学习传承。

本书对《三字经》全文进行了通俗易懂的释析，并配绘精美插图，图文并茂，以期为读者阅读了解中华传统文化提供一个优质读本。

Foreword

Three-Character Classic is a well-known introductory literacy text for students. It's written by Wang Yinglin, a scholar of the Song Dynasty and supplemented by scholars of the Ming and Qing Dynasties and the Republic of China with changes of dynasties from Song to Qing.

Although with only 1134 characters, *Three-Character Classic* is of rich content, covering ancient Chinese methods of education and learning, ethics and moral standards, astronomy and geography, the Hundred Schools of Thought and rise and fall of dynasties. To help readers learn and remember, *Three-Character Classic* is divided into five parts in sequence based on the content: filial piety and respects for elder brothers; enrich knowledge; read through classics; learn history by heart; study hard.

Children will learn the core of the Confucian rites and ethics and moral standards in the part of "filial piety and respects for elder brothers", which is the cornerstone of ancient China's moral civilization and the basis of moral education.

Children will grasp the basic living knowledge starting from knowing numbers in the part of "enrich knowledge".

Children will know the list of must read traditional cultural classics and the sequence of reading them and appreciate the splendid Chinese culture in the part of "read through classics".

Children will know the rise and fall of China's dynasties and the underlying reasons and gradually realize the tendency of establishing a united and multi-ethnic China in the part of "learn history by heart".

Children will know good examples of diligent study and be inspired by the good words and deeds of them to study hard and become celebrated and bring honor to their family in the part of "study hard".

Three-Character Classic implies systematic educational thoughts. With Confucian thoughts as its core, *Three-Character Classic* holds the belief that filial duty and respects for elder brothers is of foremost importance and moral education is required, based upon which, the book teaches children to learn the Four Books, the Five Classics, Hundred Schools of Thought and know Chinese history. It stresses the importance of perseverance and unity of theory and practice and encourages children to have lofty ideals and work hard to have both talents and high moral standard.

Three-Character Classic is written in three-character verses for easy memorization and the verses are relevant to each other by substance and numbers ranging from three talents, three cardinal guides to four seasons and four directions, from five elements, five virtues to six grains and six animals, from seven emotions and eight tones to nine degrees of kindred and ten types of righteousness.

Three-Character Classic has been praised as a mini-encyclopedia ever since its birth and it has been regarded as a classic through the ages. Its unique substance and form are of great value and worth learning.

The book is interpreted with easy-to-understand language and matched with beautiful illustrations. It's proved itself to be a top quality book for readers to understand traditional Chinese culture.

三字经

人之初	性本善	性相近	习相远
苟不教	性乃迁	教之道	贵以专
昔孟母	择邻处	子不学	断机杼
窦燕山	有义方	教五子	名俱扬
养不教	父之过	教不严	师之惰
子不学	非所宜	幼不学	老何为
玉不琢	不成器	人不学	不知义
为人子	方少时	亲师友	习礼仪
香九龄	能温席	孝于亲	所当执
融四岁	能让梨	弟于长	宜先知

首孝弟	次见闻	知某数	识某文
一而十	十而百	百而千	千而万
三才者	天地人	三光者	日月星
三纲者	君臣义	父子亲	夫妇顺
曰春夏	曰秋冬	此四时	运不穷
曰南北	曰西东	此四方	应乎中

日水火　木金土　此五行　本乎数
日仁义　礼智信　此五常　不容紊
稻粱菽　麦黍稷　此六谷　人所食
马牛羊　鸡犬豕　此六畜　人所饲
日喜怒　日哀惧　爱恶欲　七情具
匏土革　木石金　丝与竹　乃八音
高曾祖　父而身　身而子　子而孙
自子孙　至玄曾　乃九族　人之伦
父子恩　夫妇从　兄则友　弟则恭
长幼序　友与朋　君则敬　臣则忠
此十义　人所同

凡训蒙　须讲究　详训诂　明句读
为学者　必有初　小学终　至四书
论语者　二十篇　群弟子　记善言
孟子者　七篇止　讲道德　说仁义
作中庸　子思笔　中不偏　庸不易
作大学　乃曾子　自修齐　至平治
孝经通　四书熟　如六经　始可读
诗书易　礼春秋　号六经　当讲求
有连山　有归藏　有周易　三易详
有典谟　有训诰　有誓命　书之奥
我周公　作周礼　著六官　存治体

大小戴　注礼记　述圣言　礼乐备
曰国风　曰雅颂　号四诗　当讽咏
诗既亡　春秋作　寓褒贬　别善恶
三传者　有公羊　有左氏　有穀梁
经既明　方读子　撮其要　记其事
五子者　有荀扬　文中子　及老庄

经子通　读诸史　考世系　知终始
自羲农　至黄帝　号三皇　居上世
唐有虞　号二帝　相揖逊　称盛世
夏有禹　商有汤　周文武　称三王
夏传子　家天下　四百载　迁夏社
汤伐夏　国号商　六百载　至纣亡
周武王　始诛纣　八百载　最长久
周辙东　王纲坠　逞干戈　尚游说
始春秋　终战国　五霸强　七雄出
嬴秦氏　始兼并　传二世　楚汉争
高祖兴　汉业建　至孝平　王莽篡
光武兴　为东汉　四百年　终于献
魏蜀吴　争汉鼎　号三国　迄两晋
宋齐继　梁陈承　为南朝　都金陵
北元魏　分东西　宇文周　与高齐
迨至隋　一土宇　不再传　失统绪

唐高祖 起义师 除隋乱 创国基
二十传 三百载 梁灭之 国乃改
梁唐晋 及汉周 称五代 皆有由
炎宋兴 受周禅 十八传 南北混
辽与金 皆称帝 元灭金 绝宋世
莅中国 兼戎狄 九十年 国祚废
太祖兴 国大明 号洪武 都金陵
迨成祖 迁燕京 十六世 至崇祯
权阉肆 寇如林 李闯出 神器焚
清太祖 膺景命 靖四方 克大定
至世祖 乃大同 十二世 清祚终
读史者 考实录 通古今 若亲目
口而诵 心而惟 朝于斯 夕于斯

昔仲尼 师项橐 古圣贤 尚勤学
赵中令 读鲁论 彼既仕 学且勤
披蒲编 削竹简 彼无书 且知勉
头悬梁 锥刺股 彼不教 自勤苦
如囊萤 如映雪 家虽贫 学不辍
如负薪 如挂角 身虽劳 犹苦卓
苏老泉 二十七 始发愤 读书籍
彼既老 犹悔迟 尔小生 宜早思
若梁灏 八十二 对大廷 魁多士

彼既成　众称异　尔小生　宜立志
莹八岁　能咏诗　泌七岁　能赋棋
彼颖悟　人称奇　尔幼学　当效之
蔡文姬　能辨琴　谢道韫　能咏吟
彼女子　且聪敏　尔男子　当自警
唐刘晏　方七岁　举神童　作正字
彼虽幼　身已仕　有为者　亦若是
犬守夜　鸡司晨　苟不学　曷为人
蚕吐丝　蜂酿蜜　人不学　不如物
幼而学　壮而行　上致君　下泽民
扬名声　显父母　光于前　裕于后
人遗子　金满籝　我教子　惟一经
勤有功　戏无益　戒之哉　宜勉力

首重孝悌

Filial Piety and Respects for Elder Brothers

人之初　性本善　性相近　习相远
苟不教　性乃迁　教之道　贵以专
昔孟母　择邻处　子不学　断机杼
窦燕山　有义方　教五子　名俱扬
养不教　父之过　教不严　师之惰
子不学　非所宜　幼不学　老何为
玉不琢　不成器　人不学　不知义
为人子　方少时　亲师友　习礼仪
香九龄　能温席　孝于亲　所当执
融四岁　能让梨　弟于长　宜先知

　　该部分从"人之初，性本善"到"弟于长，宜先知"，讲的是教育和学习对儿童成长的重要性以及教育儿童当首先重孝悌、习礼仪。

From "people are naturally good when born" to "people should know since childhood that the younger should respect the elder", this part is about the importance of education and learning for the growth of children and the foremost importance of filial piety and respects for elder brothers and rites in children education.

1. 人之初　性本善　性相近　习相远

【释文】

　　人生命之初，本性都是向善的，只因后天学习、实践以及周围环境影响的不同，才造成了千差万别的性情。

【解析】

　　人生之初，本性向善，差别不大，到接受教育，智识渐开后，气质、禀赋就有差异了，说明生活、学习环境和教育对人的成长有着至关重要的作用。

【 Text 】

By nature, men are much alike, but in practice, they are far apart due to learning, practice and the influence of the environment.

【 Commentary 】

Men are originally good, but differ in dispositions and abilities after obtaining education. It shows that the environment and education are vital to the growth of a person.

2. 苟不教　性乃迁　教之道　贵以专

【释文】

　　如果从小不好好教育，本性就会发生变化。而教育的方法，贵在教导他专心致志、持之以恒。

【解析】

　　后天的教育对一个人的一生有举足轻重的作用，因此，在一个人成长的过程中，应及时对其施以正确的、专一的教育，否则就会养成其不良的品质和行为习惯。

【 Text 】

If not well educated, their nature will deteriorate. Focus and perseverance should be stressed in education.

【 Commentary 】

Education is of vital importance to a person. Therefore, it's important to give one the right education. Otherwise, he will develop bad characters, behaviors and habits.

3. 昔孟母　择邻处　子不学　断机杼

【释文】

从前，孟子的母亲曾三次搬家，是为了使孟子有个好的学习环境。一次孟子逃学，孟母就把织机上已经织好的布剪断来教育孟子，让孟子知道半途而废终将一事无成。

【解析】

孟子之所以能够成为历史上有名的大学问家，是和母亲的严格教育分不开的。孟母三迁的故事反映出环境在儿童教育中的重要性，断机教子的故事则强调持之以恒的重要性。孟母的教育使孟子发愤勤学，终成一代大儒。

【 Text 】

Mencius's mother moved her house three times in order to create a good learning environment for him. Once, Mencius played truant, so his mother cut the cloth that she just finished weaving to let him know that giving up halfway would lead to nothing.

【 Commentary 】

The achievements Mencius made as a great scholar in China's history should not be separated from the strict education of his mother. The story of Mencius's mother moving her house three times indicates the importance of environment in a child's education. The story of cutting finished cloth on the loom stresses the importance of perseverance. Thanks to his mother's education, Mencius worked hard and turned out to be a great scholar.

4. 窦燕山　有义方　教五子　名俱扬

【释文】

　　（五代时）窦燕山（原名窦禹钧）教育孩子很有方法，他教育的五个儿子都很有成就，名扬四海。

【解析】

　　教育必须讲究教育内容和方法。窦燕山能够使五个儿子都很有成就，是与他的教育内容和方法分不开的，也说明家庭教育对人的成长具有重要意义。

【 Text 】

Dou Yanshan (originally called Dou Yujun) of the Five Dynasties was good at teaching his children. His five sons became celebrated thanks to Dou's education.

【 Commentary 】

Good education depends on its content and methods. The achievements of Dou's five sons should be attributed to Dou's educational content and methods. It also indicates that family education is crucial to a person.

5. 养不教　父之过　教不严　师之惰

【释文】

　　做父亲的，只是供养儿女吃穿而不好好教育，那是父亲的过错。做老师的，不严格教育学生，那就是老师的失职和怠惰。

【解析】

　　对孩子严格要求是做父母和老师的本分，家庭和学校对孩子的健康成长负有重大责任，不加教育是家庭与学校的失职。

【 Text 】

It's the fault of the father if he feeds his children but not teach them. It's the fault of the teacher if he does not stringently teach his students.

【 Commentary 】

The father and the teacher should be strict with the child. Families and schools shoulder great responsibility for the healthy growth of children and it's the neglect of duty if the father and the teacher do not teach children.

6. 子不学　非所宜　幼不学　老何为

【释文】

　　小孩子不好好学习，是很不应该的。一个人倘若小时候不好好学习，到老的时候能有什么作为呢？

【解析】

　　一个人不趁年少时用功学习，长大后总是要后悔的。因此，明智的人应该趁着大好青春，抓紧时间学习，不断充实和完善自己。

【 Text 】

Children should study hard. If they do not study hard when young, how can they make their mark when they grow old?

【 Commentary 】

One will rue when growing old if he does not study hard when young. So a smart person should fully utilize his time to study hard and continuously enrich his mind and better himself when young.

7. 玉不琢　不成器　人不学　不知义

【释文】

　　玉石若是不经打磨雕琢，就不会成为精美的器物；人若是不学习，就不懂得为人处世的道理。

【解析】

　　人需要学习就如同玉需要雕琢一样，玉石只有打磨雕琢方能成为精美的玉器，人只有经过刻苦磨炼才能成为优秀的人。

【 Text 】

Jade stones will not become exquisite jade wares without chiseling. One cannot know how to behave himself well without education.

【 Commentary 】

Jade stones will not become exquisite jade wares unless chiseled. Man will not become excellent unless he works hard.

8. 为人子　方少时　亲师友　习礼仪

【释文】

　　做儿女的，从小就要亲近良师、结交益友，学习、实践为人处世的礼仪。

【解析】

　　"近朱者赤，近墨者黑"，生活在好的环境里，结交品德高尚的朋友，会受到好的影响；而生活在不良的环境里，会受到坏的影响。亲近良师，结交益友，才会受益。

【 Text 】

Children should approach good teachers and helpful friends since young so as to learn the rites of conducting themselves in society.

【 Commentary 】

He that touches the pitch shall be defiled. One will benefit from living in a good environment and making friends with those with noble character whereas one will suffer harm from living in a bad environment. One will benefit from his good teachers and helpful friends.

9. 香九龄　能温席　孝于亲　所当执

【释文】

东汉人黄香，九岁时就知道孝顺父亲，替父亲暖被窝。孝敬父母，这是每个做儿女的都应该做的事。

【解析】

百善孝为先，父母赋予我们以生命，抚育我们成长，每个人从小就应该知道做父母的不易，孝敬父母。孝亲是道德的起点，又是品行的开端。教育孩子先爱自己的父母，由此由近及远，将孝亲推衍开来，就可以爱他人，爱社会，爱国家。

【 Text 】

Although he was only nine years old, Huang Xiang of the Eastern Han Dynasty helped warm the bed of his father before his father went to bed. It's the duty of children to look after their parents.

【 Commentary 】

Filial piety is the foundation of all virtues. Our parents give us life and bring us up. We should know that parenting is not easy and we should be dutiful to them since young. Filial piety is the starting point of morality and good conduct. Children should be taught to love their parents and expand their love to others, their society and their motherland.

10. 融四岁　能让梨　弟于长　宜先知

【释文】

　　汉代人孔融四岁时，就知道把大的梨让给哥哥吃，这种敬爱兄长的美德，是每个人从小就应该知道的。

【解析】

　　友爱兄长同孝顺父母一样，也是需要从小培养的。首先学会尊敬父母兄长，才能友善地对待他人，这样家庭才会和睦，社会也才能和谐。

【 Text 】

Kong Rong of the Han Dynasty gave the bigger pear to his elder brother when at four. Every one should know the virtue of respects for elder brothers since young.

【 Commentary 】

Children should be taught to respect their elder brothers and be dutiful to their parents, based on which, they will be nice to others. By doing so, the family is in harmony and so is the society.

增广见闻

Enrich Knowledge

首孝弟	次见闻	知某数	识某文
一而十	十而百	百而千	千而万
三才者	天地人	三光者	日月星
三纲者	君臣义	父子亲	夫妇顺
曰春夏	曰秋冬	此四时	运不穷
曰南北	曰西东	此四方	应乎中
曰水火	木金土	此五行	本乎数
曰仁义	礼智信	此五常	不容紊
稻粱菽	麦黍稷	此六谷	人所食
马牛羊	鸡犬豕	此六畜	人所饲
曰喜怒	曰哀惧	爱恶欲	七情具
匏土革	木石金	丝与竹	乃八音
高曾祖	父而身	身而子	子而孙
自子孙	至玄曾	乃九族	人之伦
父子恩	夫妇从	兄则友	弟则恭
长幼序	友与朋	君则敬	臣则忠
此十义	人所同		

该部分从"首孝弟，次见闻"到"此十义，人所同"。主要讲生

活常识，先后介绍数字、四时、五行、六谷、六畜、七情、八音等日常生活必需的知识，并讲述了三纲、五常、九族、十义等礼教规范和伦理道德。

From "one should first respect his parents and the elder and then learn knowledge" to "the ten types of righteousness", this part is mainly about necessary knowledge in daily life such as numbers, four seasons, five elements, six grains, six animals, seven emotions and eight tones as well as rites and ethics and morality such as three cardinal guides, five virtues, nine degrees of kindred and ten types of righteousness.

11. 首孝弟　次见闻　知某数　识某文

　　一个人首先要学的是孝敬父母、尊敬兄长，其次是多见天下之事，多闻古今之理。还要知道基本的算术，以及识文断字。

【解析】

　　孝敬父母、友爱兄弟是做人的基础；能文会算是做人的本领。想做一个德才兼备的人，就必须从这两点做起。

【 Text 】

One should first be dutiful to his parents and show respects for his elder brothers. Apart from that, one should have wide learning and learn to do arithmetic and reading.

【 Commentary 】

Filial piety and respects for one's elder brothers is the foundation of conducting oneself in society while doing arithmetic and reading are the abilities of conducting oneself in society, both of which are important for a man with virtues and abilities.

12. 一而十 十而百 百而千 千而万

【释文】

　　天下万物的计算，都是从一开始，一到十是最基本的数字，十个十是一百，十个一百是一千，十个一千是一万，一直变化下去。

【解析】

　　一到十看起来很简单，但变化起来却无穷尽。对十进制的认识是学好数学的基础，而且几乎各个科学门类都离不开数学，应认真地从简单的数目学起，为将来学习其他知识打好基础。

【 Text 】

Counting starts from the number one. The numbers from one to ten are the basic numbers. Ten 10 are one hundred, ten 100 are one thousand and ten 1000 are ten thousand and the numbers will change in this way.

【 Commentary 】

The numbers from one to ten seem like ten simple numbers, but they can go through infinite changes. The decimal system is the foundation of mathematics and nearly all science disciplines are related to mathematics. So one should start from simple numbers and lay a solid foundation for further learning.

13. 三才者　天地人　三光者　日月星

【释文】

　　古人所谓"三才"，指的是天、地、人。古人所称"三光"，是指太阳、月亮、星星。

【解析】

　　"三才"出自《周易》，古人非常重视人在宇宙中的地位和价值，把人与天地并立，在上者为天，在下者为地，人居于中，统称"三才"。人类需要不断认识世界，包括天空中日月星辰、风雨雷电等自然现象，大地上的山川河流、花草树木、虫鱼鸟兽等自然事物，并效法天地自然之道，追求人与自然的和谐共存。

【 Text 】

The three forces mentioned by the ancients refer to the heaven, the earth and mankind and three lights mentioned by them refer to the sun, the moon and stars.

【 Commentary 】

The three forces are originally from *The Book of Changes*. Ancient people attached great importance to the position and value of mankind in the universe and put mankind along with the heaven and the earth as one of the three forces. Mankind should continuously know the world, including natural phenomena like the sun, the moon and stars, wind, rain, thunder and lightning and the nature like mountains, rivers, flowers, grass, trees, insects, fish, birds and animals and seek harmonious coexistence between the nature and mankind.

14. 三纲者　君臣义　父子亲　夫妇顺

【释文】

　　古人提出"三纲"，为君臣、父子、夫妇三种关系应当各自遵循的准则，即君臣之间讲道义，父母子女之间相亲相爱，夫妻之间和顺相处。

【解析】

　　要使君臣、父子、夫妇三者各自维持良好、和谐的关系，每个角色都要认清自己的地位，做好分内的工作，天下才能安宁、和平。

【 Text 】

The three cardinal guides proposed by the ancients refer to the principles guiding the relationship between the sovereign and the minister, the father and the son, the husband and the wife, which are the obligation between the sovereign and the minister, the love between the father and the son, the harmony between the husband and the wife.

【 Commentary 】

The sound relationship between the sovereign and the minister, the father and the son and the husband and the wife will be maintained and the whole society will be in peace and stability when each one performs his/her part well.

15. 曰春夏　曰秋冬　此四时　运不穷

【释文】

　　一年中有春、夏、秋、冬四个季节。这四个季节按次序循环往复，永不停止。

【解析】

　　春夏秋冬四个不同的季节，循环交替，运行不止。人类按季节劳作，春耕夏种秋收冬藏，因而能够繁衍生息。

【 Text 】

    There're four seasons in one year, namely, spring, summer, autumn and winter. They alternate with no end.

【 Commentary 】

    Men do their farm work in accordance with the seasons. They plough in spring, farm in summer, harvest in autumn and store food in winter.

16. 曰南北　曰西东　此四方　应乎中

【释文】

东、南、西、北，是四个方向，这四个方位，是与中央相对应而确定的。

【解析】

要有个中心点，才能定出东、西、南、北四个方位的方向。例如，人面对初升的太阳站立，那他正对的是东方，背后就是西方，左手边是北方，右手边是南方。这个人站立的地方，就是一个中心点。明辨方向，才能更好地认识自然界，不断地扩宽视野。

【 Text 】

East, south, west and north are four directions and they are determined by the center.

【 Commentary 】

The four directions of east, west, south and north are determined based upon the center. For instance, if one face the sun, his front is east and his back is west and his left is north and right is south and the place where he stands is the center. A good sense of direction will help one know more of the nature and widen his vision.

17. 曰水火　木金土　此五行　本乎数

【释文】

　　金、木、水、火、土，中国古人认为这五者可以概述物质的属性，称为"五行"。这"五行"的相生相克反映了自然界的普遍规律。

【解析】

　　"五行"的规律是相生相克，水生木，木生火，火生土，土生金，金生水；水克火，火克金，金克木，木克土，土克水。"五行"的核心内容就是生克平衡。中国古人常用"五行"来解释宇宙万物的道理及奥妙，揭示事物之间相互联系、对立统一的普遍规律。

【 Text 】

The Chinese ancients believed that metal, wood, water, fire and earth were five elements that defined properties of matter. The mutual reinforcement and neutralization of the five elements reflect the universal law of the nature.

【 Commentary 】

The five elements reinforce and counteract each other. Water reinforces wood, wood reinforces fire, fire reinforces earth, earth reinforces metal and metal reinforces water while water counteracts fire, fire counteracts metal, metal counteracts wood, wood counteracts earth and earth counteracts water. The core of the five elements is the balance between mutual reinforcement and neutralization. The Chinese ancients used the five elements to explain the law of the universe like correlation and unity of opposites.

18. 曰仁义　礼智信　此五常　不容紊

【释文】

　　仁（关爱他人）、义（持守道义）、礼（执礼守法）、智（明辨是非）、信（诚实守信），是人们说的"五常"。这五条准则，是不容许扰乱和违背的。

【解析】

　　"仁、义、礼、智、信"作为儒家文化的核心思想，在中国传承发展了几千年。这"五常"体现的智慧和价值是恒久不变的，是中华传统文化的精髓。

Humaneness, righteousness, rites, wisdom and faith are the five virtues that should not be violated.

【 Commentary 】

Humaneness, righteousness, rites, wisdom and faith are the core of Confucian thought and have been passed down for several thousands of years. The wisdom and value of the five virtues have remained unchanged as the essence of the traditional Chinese culture.

19. 稻粱菽　麦黍稷　此六谷　人所食

【释文】
　　稻米、高粱、豆子、麦子、黄米、小米，称为"六谷"，是供人食用的。

【解析】
　　稻米、黄米、小米、麦子、豆子，称为"五谷"，相传是神农氏教人们播种的。唐朝时，传说皇帝唐太宗派使臣到占城国又求得了一种谷物，也就是高粱，此时"六谷"才算齐全。民以食为天，所以我们应当重视粮食生产，还要爱惜粮食。

Rice, sorghum, beans, wheat, glutinous broomcorn millet and non glutinous broomcorn millet are six edible grains.

【 Commentary 】

Rice, wheat, beans, glutinous broomcorn millet and non glutinous broomcorn millet are five grains and legend goes that Shennong taught people how to sow them. It's said that Emperor Taizong of the Tang Dynasty sent his envoy to the kingdom of Zhancheng and brought back another grain. It was called sorghum. By then, Chinese people had six grains to eat. Food is a necessity of life, so we should attach great importance to grain production and cherish grain.

20. 马牛羊 鸡犬豕 此六畜 人所饲

【释文】

马、牛、羊、鸡、狗、猪，这六种家畜，是人类饲养的主要家畜。

【解析】

上古时期，我们的祖先不仅学会了播种农作物，而且开始把捉来的野生的马、牛、羊等留下来饲养，逐渐生息繁衍，成为家畜。

【 Text 】

Horses, cattle, sheep, chicken, dogs and pigs are six domesticated animals.

【 Commentary 】

Our ancestors learnt not only to grow crops, but also to domesticate wild horses, cattle, sheep, etc.

21. 曰喜怒　曰哀惧　爱恶欲　七情具

【释文】

欢喜、愤怒、悲伤、恐惧、喜爱、厌恶、欲求，是人所具有的七种基本情感。

【解析】

"七情"是每个人都有的，也是非常复杂的，人们需要学会妥善处理自己的情感，一定不要感情用事，走向极端。特别要理智地控制欲念，不因放纵自己的欲求而做出错事。

【 Text 】

Joy, anger, sadness, fear, fondness, hatred and desire are seven basic emotions of mankind.

【 Commentary 】

All of us are endowed with the seven emotions. They are complicated and we should learn to control our emotions to avoid wrongdoings.

22. 匏土革　木石金　丝与竹　乃八音

【释文】

　　分别用匏瓜、陶土、皮革、木块、玉石、金属、丝弦与竹管八种材料制成的乐器，各有特点，称之为"八音"。

【解析】

　　"八音"是中国古代各种乐器的总称。"八音"的代表如笙、鼓、琴、箫等，它们的音色各具特点。各种乐器合奏能使音乐产生更多的变化，使音乐更加丰富。人们可以在音乐中陶冶性情，净化心灵，培养高尚情操。

【 Text 】

Musical instruments made of gourd, pottery clay, leather, wood, jade, metal, silk string and bamboo pipes are of distinct features and called eight tones.

【 Commentary 】

Eight tones are the general name for all the ancient musical instruments. Sheng (a reed pipe wind instrument), drum, Qin (a seven-stringed plucked instrument), Xiao (a vertical bamboo flute), etc., are representatives of the eight tones and are of distinct timbres. The instrumental ensemble will produce more music changes. Music edifies people, and helps them cultivate the noble character.

23. 高曾祖　父而身　身而子　子而孙
自子孙　至玄曾　乃九族　人之伦

【释文】

　　由高祖父生曾祖父，曾祖父生祖父，祖父生父亲，父亲生我本身，我生儿子，儿子再生孙子。再接下去，就是曾孙和玄孙。从高祖父到玄孙，一共九代人，称为"九族"，是人类基本伦常关系。

【解析】

　　"九族"血脉相承，代表着家族中的长幼秩序，而尊老爱幼、仁慈孝悌，则是家庭伦理的基础。

【Text】

From great-great-grandfather, great-grandfather, grandfather, father, to us and then to our sons, grandsons, great-grandsons and great-great-grandsons, there are altogether nine generations. It's the basic family relations.

【Commentary】

The nine degrees of kindred are bonded by blood. They represent the order of birth. Respecting the elderly and caring for the young are the foundation of the familial ethics.

24. 父子恩　夫妇从　兄则友　弟则恭
长幼序　友与朋　君则敬　臣则忠
此十义　人所同

【释文】

　　父母对子女要慈爱，夫妻之间要和睦。哥哥对弟弟要友爱，弟弟对兄长则要恭敬。年长的和年幼的要注意长幼有序，朋友相处应该诚实守信。君主能体恤臣民百姓，臣子要尽忠职守。父慈、子孝、夫和、妻顺、兄友、弟恭、朋信、友义、君敬、臣忠，这"十义"是人人都应遵守的。

【解析】

　　以上所说的"十义"实际上是阐释父子、夫妇、兄弟、朋友、君臣等"五伦"的内容的，它从人伦关系的角度，规定了每个人为维护良好的人际关系应当遵守的基本道德准则。

[Text]

Parents should love their children; husband and wife should live in harmony; elder brothers should be kind to their younger ones while younger brothers should respect their elder ones. Seniority should be respected and friends should be credible. The sovereign should show solicitude for his subjects while his subjects should be loyal to the sovereign. There are ten types of righteousness: the father is loving while the son is dutiful; the husband is gentle while the wife is obedient; the elder brother is kind while the younger brother is reverent; the friend is credible and generous; the sovereign is compassionate while the minister is loyal. The ten types of righteousness should be abided by all.

[Commentary]

The ten types of righteousness elucidate the relationship between the father and the son, the husband and the wife, the elder brother and the younger ones, friends and the sovereign and the minister. They are the basic moral principles one should follow in keeping good interpersonal relationships and virtues.

通读经子

Read through Classics

凡训蒙　须讲究　详训诂　明句读
为学者　必有初　小学终　至四书
论语者　二十篇　群弟子　记善言
孟子者　七篇止　讲道德　说仁义
作中庸　子思笔　中不偏　庸不易
作大学　乃曾子　自修齐　至平治
孝经通　四书熟　如六经　始可读
诗书易　礼春秋　号六经　当讲求
有连山　有归藏　有周易　三易详
有典谟　有训诰　有誓命　书之奥
我周公　作周礼　著六官　存治体
大小戴　注礼记　述圣言　礼乐备
曰国风　曰雅颂　号四诗　当讽咏
诗既亡　春秋作　寓褒贬　别善恶
三传者　有公羊　有左氏　有穀梁
经既明　方读子　撮其要　记其事
五子者　有荀扬　文中子　及老庄

从"凡训蒙，须讲究"到"文中子，及老庄"。指示读书的次序，并介绍中国古代的重要典籍，包括四书、六经、五子等。

From "enlightenment education for children should be step by step to help children lay a solid foundation for further learning" to "Xunzi, Yangzi, Wenzhongzi, Laozi and Zhuangzi are five Zis", this part indicates the reading order and introduces to readers some important ancient classics, including the Four Books, Six Classics and Five Zis.

25. 凡训蒙 须讲究 详训诂 明句读

【释文】

儿童接受启蒙教育，要讲究循序渐进，打好基础。首先要了解字词的意思，能准确断句并把句子的意思解释清楚。

【解析】

人们在开始读书的时候必须打下一个良好的基础，文章中每一个字的读音和意义都要详细了解，一句话到哪儿停顿意思才是完整的，都要明白，这样才能正确标注标点，使段落层次分明，方便了解文意。

【 Text 】

Enlightenment education for children should be step by step to help children lay a solid foundation for further learning. Children should first learn the meaning of words and make accurate pauses in reading unpunctuated ancient writings and understand the meaning of sentences.

【 Commentary 】

One should lay a solid foundation when starting to learn. One should understand pronunciation and meaning of each character and accurate pauses of unpunctuated ancient writings, based on which, one will understand the meaning of the whole article.

26. 为学者　必有初　小学终　至四书

【释文】

　　读书求学的人，必须有一个好的开头，首先把文字音韵训诂等知识学透了，才能开始研读"四书"。

【解析】

　　小学是文字学、音韵学、训诂学的总称。《论语》《孟子》《大学》《中庸》是儒家的四部重要经典著作，合称为"四书"，它能让人了解并思考更深奥的道理。学习需要从易到难，由浅入深，循序渐进。

[Text]

One should have a good beginning in learning. One should first learn the Chinese philology, phonology and exegetics and then learn the Four Books.

[Commentary]

Lesser learning is the general term for the Chinese philology, phonology and exegetics. The Four Books are the four most important Confucian classics, including *The Analects of Confucius*, *Mencius*, *The Great Learning* and *The Doctrine of the Mean*. They help readers know abstruse philosophy and inspire them to think. Learning should start from the easier to the more advanced.

27. 论语者　二十篇　群弟子　记善言

【释文】

　　《论语》这本书，共有二十篇，是孔子的弟子及其再传弟子所编，记录了孔子与弟子们重要的、有教益的言论和对话。

【解析】

　　孔子是中国古代伟大的思想家和教育家，是儒家学派的创始人。《论语》是由孔子的弟子及再传弟子编成的，是最重要的儒家经典著作之一，是孔子和他的一些弟子的言行记录。今天的中华文化传统，《论语》是主要的思想源头之一。

【Text】

The Analects of Confucius was compiled by disciples of Confucius and their own disciples. With 20 books, it records the informative dialogues between Confucius and his disciples and their ideas.

【Commentary】

Confucius was the great thinker and educator of ancient China and the founder of Confucianism. *The Analects of Confucius* was compiled by his disciples and their own disciples. As the most important Confucian classic, it records the ideas and behaviors of Confucius and some of his disciples. The traditional Chinese culture mainly originates from *The Analects of Confucius*.

28. 孟子者　七篇止　讲道德　说仁义

《孟子》这本书，共分七篇，主要讲道德和仁义。

【解析】

　　《孟子》是又一部儒家经典著作，孟子是孔子学说的继承者，被后世尊称为"亚圣"。他主张性善论，认为人性之中本来就有善端：恻隐之心，仁之端也；羞恶之心，义之端也；辞让之心，礼之端也；是非之心，智之端也。人们应当好好地保持和培育这种本性之善。他还认为民众是最重要的，君主应当爱民、保民，实行仁政。

【 Text 】

Mencius comprises seven chapters and it's about morality and humaneness and righteousness.

【 Commentary 】

Mencius is another important Confucian classic. Mencius was the inheritor of the doctrines of Confucius and was honored as the "Second Sage". He held the belief that the original nature of all men was good. Mencius believed that compassion was the beginning of humaneness; sense of shame was the beginning of righteousness; modesty was the beginning of rites; ability of distinguishing between right and wrong was the beginning of wisdom. People should keep and cultivate their good nature. Mencius also argued that common people were of paramount importance, so the sovereign should love and protect his subjects and rule his country with benevolence.

29. 作中庸　子思笔　中不偏　庸不易

【释文】

　　作《中庸》这本书的是子思，"中"是不偏的意思，"庸"是不变的意思。

【解析】

　　子思是孔子的孙子，《中庸》的作者。他在儒家学派中承上启下，是儒学的重要传承者。《中庸》原是《礼记》中的一篇，是被宋代学人提到突出地位上来的。宋朝朱熹又作《中庸章句》，并把《中庸》和《大学》《论语》《孟子》并列称为"四书"。古人说："不偏之谓中，不易之谓庸"，"中庸"即中正和平，不偏不倚，是儒家所追求的最高理想。

[Text]

It is Zisi who wrote *The Doctrine of the Mean (Zhong Yong)*. Zhong means bent neither one way nor another, and Yong represents unchanging.

[Commentary]

Zisi, the grandson of Confucius, was the writer of *The Doctrine of the Mean*. He was an important inheritor of Confucianism. *The Doctrine of the Mean* used to be a chapter of *The Book of Rites*, but it was put in a more prominent position by Zhu Xi, the scholar in the Song Dynasty as one of the Four Books, along with *The Great Learning*, *The Analects of Confucius* and *Mencius*. According to the ancient sages, Zhong referred to bent neither one way nor another, and Yong represented unchanging. Zhong Yong, the state of balance is the loftiest ideal pursued by Confucianists.

30. 作大学　乃曾子　自修齐　至平治

【释文】

作《大学》这本书的是曾子，讲的是从修身、齐家、治国到平天下的道理。

【解析】

曾子是孔子的弟子，名曾参。《大学》本为《礼记》里面的一篇文章，后被宋朝的朱熹抽取出来与《论语》《孟子》《中庸》合称为"四书"，主要内容是讲一个人要想有所作为，首先必须学习文化知识，学习为人处世的道理，提高自身道德修养，然后治理好家庭，再进一步去治理国家，治理天下。

【Text】

It is Zengzi who wrote *The Great Learning*. It's about self-cultivation, family harmony, practice of government and world peace.

【Commentary】

Zengzi was one of the disciples of Confucius. His full name was Zeng Shen. *The Great Learning* used to be one chapter of *The Book of Rites*, yet selected by Zhu Xi, the great scholar of the Song Dynasty as one of the Four Books, along with *The Analects of Confucius*, *Mencius* and *The Doctrine of the Mean*. In the book, Zengzi held the belief that if one wanted to accomplish something, he should first acquire cultural knowledge and know how to establish himself in the society and pay attention to self-cultivation, based on which, one was able to regulate his family and then administer the country and realize the goal of world peace.

31. 孝经通　四书熟　如六经　始可读

【释文】

　　读懂了《孝经》，读熟了"四书"，才可以去读"六经"这样深奥的书。

【解析】

　　《孝经》主要论述的是孝道、孝治的思想。俗话说"百善孝为先"，孝亲是中华民族的传统美德，是人各种美德的根本，是培育幼童一切爱心的基础，把《孝经》的道理了解透彻，熟读《论语》《孟子》《大学》《中庸》四部书，才算打牢了做人做学问的基础，才可去读"六经"。

【Text】

One can read the Six Classics after reading *The Classic of Filial Piety* and the Four Books.

【Commentary】

The Classic of Filial Piety is about filial piety. It's said that filial piety is the foundation of all virtues. Filial piety is one of the traditional Chinese virtues and the foundation of nurturing a loving heart from young. One will be equipped with the basic cultural knowledge and know how to establish himself after reading *The Classic of Filial Piety* and the Four Books, based on which, one is able to read the Six Classics.

32. 诗书易　礼春秋　号六经　当讲求

【释文】

《诗经》《尚书》《周易》《礼经》《乐经》《春秋》合称为"六经"，应当认真学习研究。

【解析】

《诗经》是中国第一部诗歌总集；《尚书》是中国上古历史文献的汇编；《周易》的六十四卦反映宇宙万物的阴阳变化与发展规律，包含深刻的哲学思想；《礼经》记载古代的礼制礼仪；《春秋》是孔子根据鲁国史书修订整理而成的编年体史书。这五部书和早已失传的《乐经》合称"六经"，是儒家的重要经典。

【Text】

The Six Classics are *The Classic of Poetry, The Book of Documents, The Book of Changes, The Book of Rites, The Classic of Music* and *The Spring and Autumn Annals*. One should earnestly study the Six Classics.

【Commentary】

The Classic of Poetry is the first collection of poetry in China. *The Book of Documents* is a collection of documents and speeches alleged to have been written by rulers and officials of the early Zhou period and before. *The Book of Changes* contains a divination system of sixty-four hexagrams that reflects changes of Yin and Yang and the development law of the cosmos. It's of abstruse philosophy. *The Book of Rites* describes ancient rites, social forms and court ceremonies. *The Spring and Autumn Annals* is a chronological historical record of the State of Lu compiled by Confucius based on the historical records of the State. The five ones, along with the lost *The Classic of Music* are known as the Six Classics and they are important classics of Confucianism.

33. 有连山　有归藏　有周易　三易详

【释文】

《连山》《归藏》《周易》三部书合称"三易"，它们内容都很广博。

【解析】

《连山》是夏代之易，《归藏》是商代之易，《周易》是周代之易，三本易书都是将八卦推演为六十四卦，用来阐明天地万物生灭变化的道理，因此合称为"三易"。

【 Text 】

    Lianshan, Guicang and *Zhouyi* are together known as the three Books of Changes. They are of extensive content.

【 Commentary 】

    Lianshan is *The Book of Changes* of the Xia Dynasty; *Guicang* is *The Book of Changes* of the Shang Dynasty and *Zhouyi* is *The Book of Changes* of the Zhou Dynasty. The three books create sixty-four hexagrams based upon eight trigrams to explain changes and birth and death of the cosmos. The three books are together known as three Books of Changes.

34. 有典谟 有训诰 有誓命 书之奥

【释文】

《尚书》的文体分"典""谟""训""诰""誓""命"等类型，内容道理十分深奥。

【解析】

《尚书》是上古历史文献的汇编，记载着唐、虞、夏、商、周时代的重要史迹。它的文体分六个类别：一典，记载立国、治国的基本原则；二谟，记载计谋策略；三训，记载臣子劝谏君王的言辞；四诰，记载君王颁发的号令、通告；五誓，是起兵讨伐时的文告；六命，是君王对臣子下达的命令。《尚书》丰富翔实的材料、精深奥妙的道理，就是通过这六种特别的体式展现的。

【 Text 】

The Book of Documents is of the following types: canons, consultations, instructions, announcements, declarations and commands. It's a
book with abstruse philosophy.

【 Commentary 】

The Book of Documents is a collection of documents and speeches
alleged to have been written by rulers and officials of the semi-mythical
reign of Tang, Yu, Xia, Shang and Zhou Dynasties. It has six types:
1. Canon, recording the principles of establishing and administrating
a country. 2. Consultations, recording stratagems and strategies.
3. Instructions to the king from his ministers. 4. Announcements by the
sovereign to his people. 5. Declarations by the sovereign on the occasion
of a battle. 6. Commands by the sovereign to a specific vassal. The rich
content and abstruse philosophy are reflected through the six types.

35. 我周公　作周礼　著六官　存治体

【释文】

　　周公制作了《周礼》，其中记载着当时六官的官制以及周朝的典章制度。

【解析】

　　周公名姬旦，为西周初年杰出的政治家、军事家和思想家。周公制礼作乐，开创了周代礼乐文明。《周礼》又叫《周官》，书中将周代的礼乐制度、行政管制与朝廷组织体系完整地记录了下来，为后代保存了珍贵的资料。

【 Text 】

The Duke of Zhou wrote *The Rites of Zhou*. It records the bureaucratic and institutional system of the Zhou Dynasty.

【 Commentary 】

The full name of the Duke of Zhou was Ji Dan. He was a great statesman, strategist and thinker of the early Western Zhou Dynasty. The Duke of Zhou established the rites of Zhou, and created the yayue of Chinese classical music, starting the music and rites civilization of the Zhou Dynasty. *The Rites of Zhou* was originally known as *The Officers of Zhou*. As detailed records of the systems of music and rites, bureaucracy and organization of the Zhou Dynasty, it is a legacy for the future generations.

36. 大小戴 注礼记 述圣言 礼乐备

【释文】

汉朝的戴德、戴圣叔侄二人都曾分别选编古代各种有关礼乐制度的文章，编成《礼记》一书，阐述了圣人的言论，将礼乐制度齐备地记载了下来。

【解析】

西汉学者戴德和戴圣叔侄二人，都曾整理编纂过《礼记》，叔叔戴德编纂的称为《大戴礼记》，侄子戴圣编纂的称为《小戴礼记》。《大戴礼记》与《小戴礼记》的篇章内容虽略有不同，但都忠实地阐述了圣人的言论，对各种传统礼仪制度也讲得十分完整详细，便于后代人充分了解前代的典章制度及礼乐文化。后代通行的《礼记》指《小戴礼记》。

【 Text 】

Dai De and his nephew Dai Sheng of the Han Dynasty respectively compiled ancient writings concerning rituals and music systems into *The Books of Rites*. In their books, speeches of the ancient sages were expounded on and the rituals and music systems were recorded in details.

【 Commentary 】

Dai De and his nephew Dai Sheng of the Western Han Dynasty respectively compiled *The Books of Rites*. The book compiled by Dai De is known as *The Senior Dai's Book of Rites* while the book compiled by Dai Sheng is *The Junior Dai's Book of Rites*. The two books are slightly different in contents, but both of them faithfully expound on the speeches of the ancient sages as well as traditional ritual systems, which will help the future generations have a full understanding of the institutional systems and rites and music of the previous dynasties. The book that is popular among the future generations is *The Junior Dai's Book of Rites*.

37. 曰国风　曰雅颂　号四诗　当讽咏

【释文】

国风、大雅、小雅、颂，是《诗经》的四类内容，应当好好吟诵。

【解析】

《诗经》是中国第一部诗歌总集，收入自西周初年至春秋中叶五百多年的诗歌共305篇，又称"诗三百"，分为风、雅、颂三部分。风，指国风，是各诸侯国地区的民间歌谣；雅，是朝廷正声，分为大雅、小雅，大雅多为西周王室贵族朝会之乐，小雅多为宴飨宾客之乐；颂，分为周颂、鲁颂、商颂，是宗庙祭祀时赞颂祖先功业的乐歌。

【 Text 】

The Classic of Poetry consists of Airs of the States, Major Court Hymns, Lesser Court Hymns and Eulogies. They should be earnestly studied and well memorized.

【 Commentary 】

The Classic of Poetry is the oldest existing collection of Chinese poetry. Comprising 305 poems dating from the 11th to 7th centuries B.C., it's also known as the 300 poems. It consists of three parts: the Airs of the States, the Hymns and the Eulogies. The "Airs of the States" are shorter lyrics written in simple language. They arc generally ancient folk songs which record the voice of the common people. "Hymns" are Court Hymns and are divided into Major Court Hymns and Lesser Court Hymns. Major Court Hymns are mainly ritual songs used by the royal families and aristocracy of the Western Zhou Dynasty while the Lesser Court Hymns are used by the aristocracy at banquets. The "Eulogies" include Eulogies of Zhou, Lu and Shang. They are songs praising the founders of the Zhou Dynasty at sacrificial ceremonies.

38. 诗既亡　春秋作　寓褒贬　别善恶

【释文】

　　后来由于周朝的礼乐教化衰落，《诗经》也就没有延续下去了，所以孔子就作了《春秋》，这本书中隐含着对现实政治的褒贬以及对人们善恶行为的评价。

【解析】

　　西周以来礼坏乐崩，"诗"的传统也逐渐没落。孔子看见当时纷乱的情形，于是根据鲁国史书编撰了《春秋》，书中以隐喻的方式评论史事，或是给予赞扬，或是给予指责，辨明了各诸侯国行为的是非善恶。

【 Text 】

The Classic of Poetry fell into decay due to the decline of rites and music since the Zhou Dynasty. So Confucius compiled *The Spring and Autumn Annals* which contains praise and criticism of the current politics and judgment on good and bad deeds.

【 Commentary 】

The tradition of poetry fell into decay due to the decline of rites and music since the Western Zhou Dynasty. On seeing the chaos, Confucius compiled *The Spring and Autumn Annals* bascd on the historical records of the State of Lu. In the book, Confucius employed metaphors to praise or criticize historical events and pointed out good and bad deeds done by vassal states.

39. 三传者　有公羊　有左氏　有穀梁

【释文】

　　解释《春秋》的书，有《公羊传》《左传》和《穀梁传》。

【解析】

　　《公羊传》，相传为齐国人公羊高所作；《左传》，相传为鲁国人左丘明写成；《穀梁传》，相传为鲁国人穀梁赤所著。"三传"分别从不同角度注解《春秋》这部书，后均成儒家重要经典。

【 Text 】

The Commentary of Gongyang, The Commentary of Zuo and *The Commentary of Guliang* are three commentaries on *The Spring and Autumn Annals.*

【 Commentary 】

It is said that *The Commentary of Gongyang* was written by Gongyang Gao of the State of Qi; *The Commentary of Zuo* was written by Zuo Qiuming of the State of Lu and *The Commentary of Guliang* was written by Guliang Chi of the State of Lu. As commentaries on *The Spring and Autumn Annals* from different perspectives, the three books have become important Confucian classics.

40. 经既明 方读子 撮其要 记其事

【释文】

　　"四书""六经"都读熟了，弄明白了，就可以阅读诸子百家的著作了。阅读的时候要明白其要义，并且要记住事件的本末因果。

【解析】

　　"四书""六经"是儒家最重要的经典，这些重要典籍都读熟之后，就可以开始接触诸子百家的思想了。这些记载各家各派思想言行的书，统称为"子书"。"子书"数量庞大，内容包罗万象，因此要掌握其要义，且应仔细分辨读过的内容，记住事件的因果本末。

【 Text 】

One can read writings by the Hundred Schools of Thought after finishing reading the Four Books and the Six Classics. When reading, one should grasp the gist and remember the cause and effect of the events.

【 Commentary 】

The Four Books and the Six Classics are the most important classics of Confucianism. One is able to read writings by the Hundred Schools of Thought after finishing reading them. The writings by the Hundred Schools of Thought are of large quantity and rich content, so one should grasp their gist and memorize the cause and effect of the events.

41. 五子者　有荀扬　文中子　及老庄

【释文】

　　五子是指荀子、扬子、文中子、老子和庄子。

【解析】

　　荀子，即战国时期荀况，著有《荀子》一书，是继孔孟之后儒家的又一重要代表；扬子，即西汉扬雄，著有《太玄》《法言》等；文中子，即隋代王通，著有《中说》等；老子，相传为春秋末年李耳，是道家学派的创始人，主张无为而治，著有《道德经》；庄子，即战国时期庄周，是道家学派的另一代表人物，与老子并称"老庄"，著有《庄子》一书。

【 Text 】

Xunzi, Yangzi, Wenzhongzi, Laozi and Zhuangzi are five Zis.

【 Commentary 】

Xunzi refers to Xun Kuang of the Warring States Period. He wrote the book *Xunzi* and was another important representative of Confucianism after Confucius and Mencius. Yangzi refers to Yang Xiong of the Western Han Dynasty, who wrote *Great Mystery* and *Exemplary Sayings*. Wenzhongzi refers to Wang Tong of the Sui Dynasty, who wrote *The Sayings of Wenzhongzi*. Laozi is Li Er of the Spring and Autumn Period. He was the founder of Taoism and held the belief of governing by doing nothing that goes against nature. He was known as the author of *Tao Te Ching*. Zhuangzi refers to Zhuang Zhou of the Warring States Period, who wrote *Zhuangzi*. As another representative of Taoism, Zhuangzi was as famous as Laozi.

熟读诸史

Learn History by Heart

经子通　读诸史　考世系　知终始
自羲农　至黄帝　号三皇　居上世
唐有虞　号二帝　相揖逊　称盛世
夏有禹　商有汤　周文武　称三王
夏传子　家天下　四百载　迁夏社
汤伐夏　国号商　六百载　至纣亡
周武王　始诛纣　八百载　最长久
周辙东　王纲坠　逞干戈　尚游说
始春秋　终战国　五霸强　七雄出
嬴秦氏　始兼并　传二世　楚汉争
高祖兴　汉业建　至孝平　王莽篡
光武兴　为东汉　四百年　终于献
魏蜀吴　争汉鼎　号三国　迄两晋
宋齐继　梁陈承　为南朝　都金陵
北元魏　分东西　宇文周　与高齐
迨至隋　一土宇　不再传　失统绪
唐高祖　起义师　除隋乱　创国基
二十传　三百载　梁灭之　国乃改
梁唐晋　及汉周　称五代　皆有由
炎宋兴　受周禅　十八传　南北混
辽与金　皆称帝　元灭金　绝宋世

莅中国　兼戎狄　九十年　国祚废
太祖兴　国大明　号洪武　都金陵
迨成祖　迁燕京　十六世　至崇祯
权阉肆　寇如林　李闯出　神器焚
清太祖　膺景命　靖四方　克大定
至世祖　乃大同　十二世　清祚终
读史者　考实录　通古今　若亲目
口而诵　心而惟　朝于斯　夕于斯

从"经子通，读诸史"到"朝于斯，夕于斯"，这部分通过通俗简明的语言梳理出一条清晰且便于记忆的中国历史发展的基本线索，其中蕴含着丰富的历史故事及文化内涵。

From "read history books after finishing reading classics and writings of the Hundred Schools of Thought" to "read aloud and memorize what one's leant single-mindedly in the morning and in the evening", this part is about the history of China and tells readers historical stories and their underlying cultural connotations.

42. 经子通　读诸史　考世系　知终始

【释文】

经书和子书读熟了以后，再读史书。读史时要考究各朝代的更替传承关系，明白它们盛衰的过程和原因。

【解析】

中国是一个历史悠久的文明古国，经历了众多王朝的更替，研读史书的时候要注意历代王朝的次序，深入研究其中的关系，才能明白国家盛衰更替的道理，掌握治国的方法和原则。

【Text】

One is able to read history books after finishing reading classics and writings of the Hundred Schools of Thought. When reading them, one should know the changes of dynasties and the course of and reasons for their rise and fall.

【Commentary】

China is an ancient civilization with a long history. It has undergone changes of a lot of dynasties. When reading history books, one should know the sequence of the dynasties and reasons for their rise and fall and the ways and principles of administering a country.

43. 自羲农　至黄帝　号三皇　居上世

【释文】

　　自伏羲氏、神农氏到黄帝，这三位帝王被后人尊称为"三皇"，他们都处在远古时代。

【解析】

　　传说，伏羲氏教人驯养禽畜、结网渔猎，并首创文字，绘制八卦；神农氏则播种五谷、尝遍百草，是传说中农业和医学的开创者；黄帝是传说中的中原各族的共同祖先和人文始祖。

【Text】

Fuxi, Shennong and the Yellow Emperor were the three Sovereigns. They lived in the prehistoric times.

【Commentary】

Legend goes that Fuxi taught people to domesticate animals and go fishing with nets and created characters and eight trigrams. Shennong was the legendary founder of agriculture and medicine. The Yellow Emperor was the ancestor of people of the Central China and initiator of Chinese civilization.

44. 唐有虞　号二帝　相揖逊　称盛世

【释文】

　　唐尧和虞舜称为"二帝"，尧把帝位禅让给舜，在两位帝王治理下，天下太平。

【解析】

　　唐尧和虞舜并称"尧舜"，是远古部落联盟的首领，古史传说中的圣明君主。

【 Text 】

Yao and Shun were two emperors. Yao abdicated the throne to Shun. The world was in peace under the reign of the two emperors.

【 Commentary 】

Yao and Shun were heads of the tribal confederation in the prehistoric times. They were enlightened legendary rulers.

45. 夏有禹　商有汤　周文武　称三王

【释文】

夏朝的开国君主是禹，商朝的开国君主是汤，周朝有文王和武王。三个朝代的开国之君被后人称为"三王"。

【解析】

禹因治水有功继承王位；商汤任用贤能，除残去虐；周文王经天纬地，在位期间国泰民安，他的儿子周武王继承父亲遗志，伐暴救民。他们都是德才兼备的好君王，勤于政事，爱护百姓。"三王"被后世君王奉为典范。

【 Text 】

The first emperor of the Xia Dynasty was Yu and the first emperor of the Shang Dynasty was Tang and the King Wen and the King Wu were from the Zhou Dynasty. The founding kings of the three dynasties were called "Three Kings" by the future generations.

【 Commentary 】

Yu ascended the throne due to his feats in fighting against flood. Tang promoted those with talents and virtues and removed the cruel. King Wen of Zhou was a talented ruler and his state was in prosperity and peace during his reign. His son King Wu of Zhou followed his father's step to remove the cruel and help commoners. They were all good rulers with both talents and virtues. They were diligent in handling state affairs and took good care of their subjects. Therefore, they were honored as exemplary sovereigns by the future generations.

46. 夏传子　家天下　四百载　迁夏社

【释文】

　　禹把帝位传给自己的儿子，从此帝位的继承就由禅让制变为世袭制。经过四百多年，夏被汤灭掉，从而结束了它的统治。

【解析】

　　大禹年老时，将王位传给了儿子夏启，从此，尧舜以来的禅让制度被父传子的世袭制度所代替，天下为一家所有，世代相传。

【Text】

Yu passed the throne on to his son and since then, the imperial succession changed from voluntary abdication to hereditary succession. The Xia Dynasty was overthrown by Tang after ruling for over 400 years.

【Commentary】

Yu passed his throne on to his son Qi when old. Since then, the voluntary abdication system adopted by Yao and Shun was replaced by the hereditary succession system.

47. 汤伐夏　国号商　六百载　至纣亡

【释文】

商汤讨伐夏桀，建立了商朝，经过了六百年，到纣王时商朝灭亡。

【解析】

商朝又称殷商，是中国历史上继夏朝之后的第二个朝代，处于奴隶制鼎盛时期。后因纣王统治残暴，周武王顺应民意讨伐纣王，大败商朝军队，纣王自焚而死，商朝灭亡。

【 Text 】

　　Tang overthrew the Xia Dynasty and founded the Shang Dynasty.
After ruling for 600 years, the Shang Dynasty perished during the reign
of King Zhou.

【 Commentary 】

　　The Shang Dynasty was the second dynasty after the Xia Dynasty.
It was in the prime of the slavery system. The last sovereign of the
Shang Dynasty was King Zhou, who was very cruel. King Wu of Zhou
complied with the popular wish of the people to mount an expedition to
the Shang Dynasty and defeated the army of the Shang Dynasty. King
Zhou burned himself to death and the Shang Dynasty perished.

48. 周武王 始诛纣 八百载 最长久

【释文】

　　周武王起兵灭掉商朝，使纣王自焚而死，建立周朝，周朝的历史最长，前后延续了八百年。

【解析】

　　周武王是西周王朝开国君主，他雄才大略，率领军队讨伐商朝，表现出卓越的军事、政治才能，成了中国历史上的一代明君。周朝分为"西周"与"东周"两个时期，是中国第三个也是最后一个世袭奴隶制王朝。

【 Text 】

King Wu of Zhou overthrew the Shang Dynasty and King Zhou burned himself to death. The Zhou Dynasty was founded. Lasting 800 years, the Zhou Dynasty enjoyed the longest reign in history.

【 Commentary 】

King Wu of Zhou was the founding monarch of the Western Zhou Dynasty. He was a man with great talent and bold vision. During his expedition against the Shang Dynasty, he showed his great military prowess and statesmanship. King Wu of Zhou was an enlightened monarch in Chinese history. The Zhou Dynasty was divided into two periods: the Western Zhou Dynasty and the Eastern Zhou Dynasty and it was the third and also the last dynasty with slavery system and hereditary succession in China.

49. 周辙东 王纲坠 逞干戈 尚游说

【释文】

　　自从周平王东迁国都后，周王朝的纲纪就败坏了。诸侯国之间肆意以武力解决争端，社会上崇尚游说纵横之士。

【解析】

　　周王室衰落，使各诸侯失去了控制，诸侯们不再听从周天子的号令，为了争夺霸主的地位，战争不断。在乱世中，有才能的人各凭本事游说四方，到处发表自己的见解和政治主张，希望被诸侯们采用。

【Text】

The social order and law of the Zhou Dynasty were disrupted after the King Ping of Zhou moved his capital eastward. Vassal states arbitrarily resorted force to solve their disputes and political strategists were popular.

【Commentary】

The Zhou royal family declined, so its vassal states did not obey the sovereign of the Zhou Dynasty. Wars emerged one after another as rulers of vassal states fought for supremacy. In the troubled times, political strategists traveled far and wide to express their views, hoping rulers of vassal states would adopt their ideas.

50. 始春秋　终战国　五霸强　七雄出

【释文】

东周分春秋、战国两个时期。春秋时有齐桓公、晋文公、楚庄王、吴王阖闾、越王勾践，号称五霸。战国七雄分别为齐、楚、燕、韩、赵、魏、秦。

【解析】

春秋时期诸侯混战，公元前494年，吴王夫差攻克越国，越王勾践成为亡国之君，被带到吴国，受尽苦难和凌辱。被赦回越后，为了提醒自己不忘雪耻，他在坐卧的地方吊着个苦胆，吃饭、睡觉之前都要尝一尝。最后，终于由弱变强，灭掉吴国。

【Text】

The Eastern Zhou was divided into two periods: the Spring and Autumn Period and the Warring States Period. The Duke Huan of Qi, Duke Wen of Jin, King Zhuang of Chu, King Helü of Wu and King Goujian of Yue were the five overlords in the Spring and Autumn Period. Qi, Chu, Yan, Han, Zhao, Wei and Qin were the seven Warring States.

【Commentary】

Vassal states fought with each other in the Spring and Autumn Period. The King Fuchai of Wu invaded the State of Yue and the King Goujian of Yue was captured and brought to the State of Wu in 494 B.C. King Goujian went through great sufferings and humiliation. He tasted gall before eating and sleeping to remind him of revenge after being sent back to the State of Yue. Finally, his state became stronger and conquered the State of Wu.

51. 嬴秦氏　始兼并　传二世　楚汉争

【释文】

秦始皇嬴政统一六国，建立秦朝。秦传到二世胡亥，天下又开始大乱，最后，形成楚汉相争的局面。

【解析】

秦王朝是中国历史上第一个中央集权制王朝，秦国国君嬴政自称为"始皇帝"。秦始皇去世后，他的儿子胡亥继承皇位。由于施行残暴统治，加上宦官专权，秦二世继位后不过短短三年时间，秦朝统治就被推翻了。秦朝灭亡后，群雄并起，其中以西楚霸王项羽与汉王刘邦实力最强大。

【 Text 】

Ying Zheng, the first emperor of Qin unified China after conquering the other six states and established the Qin Dynasty. There was great disorder during the reign of the second emperor Huhai and eventually, two powers Chu and Han stood out from the rest and fought with each other for supremacy.

【 Commentary 】

The Qin Dynasty was the first centralized dynasty in Chinese history, so Ying Zheng was called the first emperor. His son Huhai ascended the throne after his death. Thanks to his cruel ruling and eunuchs' monopoly of power, the second emperor of Qin was in reign for just three short years before being overthrown. After the destruction of the Qin Dynasty, warlords emerged and among whom, Xiang Yu, the King of Western Chu and Liu Bang, the King of Han were the two most powerful.

52. 高祖兴　汉业建　至孝平　王莽篡

【释文】

　　汉高祖刘邦打败了项羽，建立汉朝。汉朝的帝位传到孝平帝时，被王莽篡权。

【解析】

　　公元前202年，刘邦在楚汉之争中最后胜出，战胜项羽，建立汉朝。到汉平帝时，王莽靠着外戚的力量掌握了大权。他杀了平帝，篡夺了帝位，建立了新朝。

【 Text 】

    Liu Bang defeated Xiang Yu and founded the Han Dynasty. He was the Emperor Gaozu of Han. When the Emperor Xiaoping was in reign, Wang Mang usurped the power.

【 Commentary 】

    Liu Bang defeated Xiang Yu and founded the Han Dynasty in 202 B.C., and when the Emperor Xiaoping was in reign, Wang Mang usurped the throne by killing the emperor and created the Xin Dynasty.

53. 光武兴　为东汉　四百年　终于献

【释文】

　　汉光武帝刘秀建立东汉政权，复兴汉室。从汉高祖刘邦开始，汉朝延续四百年，到汉献帝的时候灭亡。

【解析】

　　王莽建立新朝后，人民无法安稳生活，于是国家重新陷入纷争局面。王莽在混战中被杀，新朝灭亡。刘秀最终打败其他势力，光复汉室，史称东汉，刘秀就是汉光武帝。

【 Text 】

Liu Xiu, the Emperor Guangwu restored the Han Dynasty by founding the Eastern Han Dynasty. The Han Dynasty lasted for four hundred years from Liu Bang, the Emperor Gaozu to the Emperor Xian.

【 Commentary 】

People lived in disorder after Wang Mang established the Xin Dynasty. The whole country was in a state of war and Wang Mang was killed in a tangled fight and his Xin Dynasty perished. Liu Xiu defeated other forces and restored the Han Dynasty by founding the Eastern Han Dynasty, and he was known as the Emperor Guangwu.

54. 魏蜀吴　争汉鼎　号三国　迄两晋

【释文】

东汉末年，魏、蜀、吴争夺天下，形成三国相争的局面。后来司马炎逼迫魏王退位，重新统一天下，建立了晋朝，晋又分为西晋和东晋两个时期。

【解析】

东汉末年，天下大乱，赤壁之战奠定了三国鼎立的局面：曹操占据了北方绝大部分地区，他的儿子曹丕取代汉献帝自立为帝，国号"魏"；刘备占据西南，国号"汉"，史称"蜀汉"；孙权统治了长江下游地区，国号"吴"。魏、蜀、吴三分天下，史称三国时代。

【 Text 】

The Kingdom of Wei, the Kingdom of Shu and the Kingdom of Wu competed for supremacy over China at the end of the Eastern Han Dynasty, known in the history as the Three Kingdoms Period. Sima Yan took the place of the emperor of Wei by compulsion and united the whole nation and established the Jin Dynasty. The Jin Dynasty was divided into the Western Jin and the Eastern Jin.

【 Commentary 】

The whole nation was in chaos at the end of the Eastern Han Dynasty and the Battle of Red Cliff created the Three Kingdoms Period. Cao Cao occupied most of the northern China and his son Cao Pi replaced the Emperor Xian of Han and proclaimed himself the emperor and founded the Kingdom of Wei. Liu Bei occupied southwestern China and founded the Kingdom of Han, historically known as Shuhan. Sun Quan occupied the lower reaches of Yangtze River and founded the Kingdom of Wu. This period was called the Three Kingdoms Period.

55. 宋齐继　梁陈承　为南朝　都金陵

【释文】

　　晋朝之后，在南方相继兴起的是宋、齐、梁、陈。它们被统称为"南朝"，都城都在金陵。

【解析】

　　宋、齐、梁、陈四朝都把国都设在金陵，国土都局限于长江以南地区，统治时间又都非常短暂，于是，历史上合称为"南朝"。

【 Text 】

Song, Qi, Liang and Chen rose in the southern China after the end of the Jin Dynasty. With their capital in Jinling, they were called the Southern Dynasties.

【 Commentary 】

Because Song, Qi, Liang and Chen had their capital in Jinling, and they were all located in the south of the Yangtze River and short-lived, they were grouped together as the Southern Dynasties.

56. 北元魏　分东西　宇文周　与高齐

【释文】

　　与南朝同时存在的统治北方的王朝统称为"北朝"，首先是北魏，北魏后来又分裂成东魏和西魏，西魏被宇文氏篡了位，建立了北周；东魏被高洋篡了位，建立了北齐。

【解析】

　　北魏孝文帝改革，是中国历史上的一件大事。他改鲜卑姓为汉姓，改易服装，使鲜卑族与中原士族通婚，对于巩固中国北方的统一，起了积极的作用。

【Text】

Dynasties that ruled the northern China and existed at the same period of the Southern Dynasties were grouped together as the Northern Dynasties. The first dynasty was Northern Wei, which was later divided into Eastern and Western Weis. Yuwen Jue seized the throne of power from Emperor Gong of Western Wei, establishing the Northern Zhou Dynasty while Gao Yang forced the Eastern Wei emperor to abdicate in favor of his claim to the throne, establishing the Northern Qi Dynasty.

【Commentary】

The reforms made by the Emperor Xiaowen of Northern Wei were great historical events. He had the Xianbei elites apply Chinese surnames to their families, don Chinese clothing and encouraged the clans of high-ranking Xianbei and Chinese families to intermarry. His sinification program greatly promoted the unification of the northern China.

57. 迨至隋　一土宇　不再传　失统绪

【释文】

到了隋朝，天下再度统一。可是隋朝只经过一次帝王传位便灭亡了。

【解析】

杨坚起兵东征西讨，结束了南北朝长期分裂的局面，重新统一中国。杨坚建立隋朝，史称隋文帝。文帝死后，其子炀帝继位。因隋炀帝对内大兴土木，穷奢极侈，对外穷兵黩武，攻伐劫掠，导致隋末天下大乱，群雄并起，隋朝也随之很快灭亡。

【 Text 】

The whole nation was united during the Sui Dynasty, but the Sui Dynasty perished after the throne was passed onto the second emperor.

【 Commentary 】

Yang Jian united the whole nation and founded the Sui Dynasty. He was known as the Emperor Wen of Sui and his son the Emperor Yang ascended the throne after his death. The Emperor Yang started many expensive construction projects, lived a life of decadent luxury and became embroiled in several costly wars. What he did led to great chaos and the destruction of the Sui Dynasty.

58. 唐高祖　起义师　除隋乱　创国基

【释文】

　　唐高祖李渊，发起仁义之师，推翻了隋朝的暴政，开创了唐朝的基业。

【解析】

　　隋炀帝好大喜功、荒淫残暴，百姓生活在水深火热之中，纷纷起义。最后，李渊率领的军队脱颖而出，推翻了已处于土崩瓦解的隋朝，李渊登基，世谓唐高祖，开创唐朝基业。

【 Text 】

Li Yuan, the Emperor of Gaozu of Tang overthrew the tyrannical rule of the emperor of Sui Dynasty and founded the Tang Dynasty.

【 Commentary 】

The Emperor Yang of Sui was a tyrant and lived a life of decadent luxury. The commoners were plunged into an abyss of suffering and had to rise up against him. The army led by Li Yuan stood out among them and overthrew the crumbling Sui Dynasty. Li Yuan founded Tang Dynasty and became the Emperor of Gaozu of Tang.

59. 二十传　三百载　梁灭之　国乃改

【释文】

　　唐朝传承二十个皇帝，历经近三百年。最后被后梁所灭，于是改换了朝代。

【解析】

　　唐朝是中国古代国力最强盛的朝代之一。唐太宗李世民开创"贞观之治"，唐玄宗统治的前期史称"开元盛世"，但后期却发生了"安史之乱"，唐朝从此开始衰落，后来又经历了几次大规模的动乱，公元907年，朱温代唐称帝，改国号为"梁"，为了与南北朝时期的梁朝相区别，史称"后梁"。

【 Text 】

Tang Dynasty was extinguished by Liang after ruling nearly 300 years of history with altogether 20 emperors.

【 Commentary 】

China had ever been the strongest country in the world during the Tang Dynasty. Li Shimin, the Emperor Taizong of Tang, created Prosperity of Zhenguan. The early stage of the reign of Emperor Xuanzong was known as Heyday of Kaiyuan whereas in the later years of Emperor Xuanzong, An Lushan launched a revolt against the Tang Dynasty with Shi Siming and Tang Dynasty declined since then. Several large-scale revolts happened during the reign of the following emperors. In 907, Zhu Wen changed the state title to "Liang", which known as "Later Liang" so as to distinguish it from the Liang of the Southern and Northern Dynasties. Zhu Wen made himself Emperor Taizu.

60. 梁唐晋　及汉周　称五代　皆有由

【释文】

　　后梁、后唐、后晋、后汉和后周，统称作"五代"，"五代"之称都有来由。

【解析】

　　"五代"是中国历史上一个纷乱割据的时期，由唐末的藩镇割据演变而来。这些朝代名都是以前有过的，所以各冠一个"后"字来区别。

【 Text 】

Later Liang, Later Tang, Later Jin, Later Han and Later Zhou were grouped as Five Dynasties.

【 Commentary 】

The Five Dynasties were in a period of chaos and havoc. They were called Later because their names were used by the previous dynasties.

61. 炎宋兴　受周禅　十八传　南北混

【释文】

　　赵匡胤接受了后周"禅让"的帝位，建立宋朝。宋朝传了十八个皇帝之后，北方的少数民族南下侵扰，结果又成了南北混战的局面。

【解析】

　　后周的恭帝七岁即位，大权便落入了禁军将领赵匡胤手中，他与部下合力演出"黄袍加身"，后周皇帝知道大势已去，只好将帝位禅让给他。赵匡胤登基后，改国号为"宋"，就是宋太祖。宋朝是中国古代历史上经济、文化教育与科学创新高度繁荣的时代。

【 Text 】

The last emperor of the Later Zhou abdicated the throne and handed over the crown to Zhao Kuangyin, who established the Song Dynasty. During the reign of the 18th emperor, the Song Dynasty was invaded by northern nomads and the nation was in turbulence.

【 Commentary 】

When Emperor Gong of Later Zhou was at seven, his power fell into the hands of Zhao Kuangyin, the Chief of the Palace Troops, who launched a coup d'état at Chen Bridge with his troops. Knowing that the end had come, the emperor of Later Zhou abdicated and handed over the crown to Zhao. Zhao Kuangyin changed the title of the reigning dynasty into Song and he was known as Emperor Taizu of Song. The Song Dynasty was the heyday of economic, cultural and educational development and technological innovation in the history of China.

62. 辽与金　皆称帝　元灭金　绝宋世

【释文】

　　北方的辽人、金人和蒙古人都建立了国家，自称皇帝，最后蒙古人灭了金国之后，又灭了宋朝。

【解析】

　　辽是中国历史上契丹族建立的政权，金是中国历史上女真族建立的政权，它们的建立极大地推动了中华民族大融合的历史进程。蒙古族成吉思汗统一各部落，灭掉金朝，于公元 1206 年建国，他就是元太祖。公元 1271 年忽必烈改国号为"元"，1279 年灭掉南宋，再次统一中国。

[Text]

The empires of Liao, Jin and Mongol were established in northern China. The Mongols destroyed the Jin Dynasty and then the Song Dynasty.

[Commentary]

The Liao Dynasty was founded by the Khitan people while the Jin Dynasty was founded by the Jurchen people. The two empires greatly accelerated the ethnic integration of China. Genghis Khan of the Mongol united the Mongol tribes and founded the Mongol Empire in 1206 and was known as Emperor Taizu of Yuan. Under the reign of Genghis' the third son of Genghlis khan, Ögedei Khan, the Mongols destroyed the weakened Jin Dynasty. Kublai changed the dynastic name into Yuan in 1271 and reunited China in 1279 after destroying the Southern Song Dynasty.

63. 莅中国 兼戎狄 九十年 国祚废

【释文】

　　元朝入主中原，吞并了各民族政权，它的政权只维持了九十年就结束了。

【解析】

　　蒙古人入主中原，又吞并了西方和北方各少数民族政权，统一全国。元朝疆域空前广阔，它的全盛时期，国力强盛。元朝统治期间四处征战，导致民不聊生，结果只维持了短短九十年的时间就被农民起义推翻了。

【 Text 】

The Yuan Dynasty was established to rule the whole China after annexting the other regimes, but it lasted for only 90 years.

【 Commentary 】

The Mongols reunified China and established the Yuan Dynasty. The Yuan Dynasty was of vast territory and strong power in its heyday, but its rulers were addicted to military conquests, causing hunger and poverty among the commoners. It was overthrown by peasants' revolts after a short ruling history of 90 years.

64. 太祖兴　国大明　号洪武　都金陵

【释文】

明太祖朱元璋起义，建立明朝，年号洪武，定都金陵（今南京）。

【解析】

明朝是中国历史上最后一个由汉族建立的大一统封建王朝。明朝时期手工业和商品经济发达、经济繁荣，出现了资本主义萌芽，文化艺术呈现世俗化趋势，如小说的大量涌现。

【 Text 】

Zhu Yuanzhang rose up and founded the Ming Dynasty, making his capital at Jinling (now known as Nanjing, the capital of Jiangsu Province). He was Emperor Taizu and his title of reign was Hongwu.

【 Commentary 】

The Ming Dynasty was the last centralized feudal dynasty founded by Han people. The Ming Dynasty boasted developed handicraft industry and commodity economy and economic prosperity and the seeds of capitalism. With popularization of culture and arts, novels emerged in large numbers.

65. 迨成祖　迁燕京　十六世　至崇祯

【释文】

明成祖即位后，把国都由南京迁到燕京（今北京）。明朝共传了十六世，直到崇祯皇帝为止。

【解析】

明太祖的第四个儿子燕王朱棣不满自己的侄儿建文帝继位，于是率军发动政变。建文帝在战乱中下落不明，朱棣夺取了皇位，就是明成祖。崇祯十七年（1644）正月，李自成在西安建立大顺政权，年号永昌；三月攻克北京，崇祯帝走投无路，自缢于煤山（今北京景山），明朝灭亡。

【 Text 】

When Emperor Chengzu of Ming ascended the throne, he moved the capital from Jinling to Yanjing (now known as Beijing). The Ming Dynasty was ruled by 16 emperors and ended at Emperor Chongzhen.

【 Commentary 】

Zhu Di, the fourth son of Emperor Taizu of Ming was resentful that his nephew, Emperor Jianwen succeeded to the throne and staged a coup d'état. Emperor Jianwen was missing in the chaos and Zhu Di seized the throne and became Emperor Chengzu. Li Zicheng established the Dashun regime with Yongchang as the reigning title in 1644 and conquered Beijing in March of the same year. Emperor Chongzhen committed suicide by hanging himself on Meishan (now known as Jingshan in Beijing) and the Ming Dynasty fell.

66. 权阉肆　寇如林　李闯出　神器焚

【释文】

　　明朝末年，宦官专权，天下大乱，老百姓纷纷起义，以闯王李自成为首的起义军攻破北京，迫使崇祯皇帝自杀，明朝灭亡。

【解析】

　　明末宦官专权，带来了政治的腐败，百姓怨声载道，全国各地纷纷爆发了大规模的农民起义，众多起义军中以闯王李自成的势力最大，他率领的起义军攻破北京，迫使崇祯帝上吊自杀，明朝统治结束。

【Text】

Eunuchs monopolized the state power and the whole nation was in chaos at the end of the Ming Dynasty. The commoners rose up. Beijing was sacked by a coalition of rebel forces led by Li Zicheng and the last Ming ruler, Emperor Chongzhen was forced to commit suicide, marking the official end of the dynasty.

【Commentary】

Eunuchs monopolized power during the late Ming period, giving rise to political corruption. Grumblings of the people were heard everywhere and large-scale peasants' revolts were rampant. Li Zicheng, nicknamed Dashing King, was the most powerful among all the rebels. Li's rebels sacked the Ming capital of Beijing and forced Emperor Chongzhen to commit suicide, marking the end of the Ming Dynasty.

67. 清太祖　膺景命　靖四方　克大定

【释文】

　　清太祖努尔哈赤上顺天命，平定四方，安定了女真各部。

【解析】

　　这四句讲的是清太祖统一女真各部的事情。努尔哈赤经营四十多年，统一女真各部，于万历四十四年（1616）建立后金。清朝建立后，被追尊为清太祖。

【 Text 】

Nurhaci followed the mandate of heaven to unify Jurchen tribes.

【 Commentary 】

Nurhaci founded Later Jin in 1616 and during his reign for over 40 years, he unified Jurchen clans . He was revered as Emperor Taizu of Qing after the establishment of the Qing Dynasty.

68. 至世祖　乃大同　十二世　清祚终

【释文】

到了清世祖顺治帝，天下一统。清帝传至十二世，国运告终。

【解析】

顺治元年（1644），清兵入关，建都北京，统一中国，自清太祖起清代共历十二帝。清朝是中国历史上第二个由少数民族建立的统一政权，也是中国最后一个封建王朝，对中国历史产生了深远影响。

【 Text 】

The whole nation was reunified during the reign of the Shunzhi Emperor (posthumous name was Shizu) of Qing. The Qing Dynasty collapsed during the reign of the 12th emperor.

【 Commentary 】

Qing armies established their capital in Beijing and unified the whole nation in 1644, the first year of the reign of Emperor Shunzhi. The Qing Dynasty was ruled by 12 emperors starting from Emperor Taizu. The Qing Dynasty was the second centralized dynasty founded by ethnic minority groups and the last imperial dynasty in China. It was of profound influence on China's history.

69. 读史者　考实录　通古今　若亲目

【释文】

　　研读历史的人还要考察历代实录，通晓古今历史事件，就好像是自己亲眼所见一样。

【解析】

　　中国是一个历史悠久的文明古国，不仅有悠久的历史，也有悠久的史学传统。阅读史书要注意进一步查找历史资料，对照参考，从多个角度去理解历史事件。

【 Text 】

Those who study history should familiarize themselves with historical records and historical events.

【 Commentary 】

China is an ancient civilization with a long history and good traditions of historiography. When reading historical records, one should cross reference historical information and understand historical events from different perspectives.

70. 口而诵　心而惟　朝于斯　夕于斯

【释文】

读书要嘴里念，心里想，专心致志。早、晚都应这样做。

【解析】

中国的古文是讲究韵律和节奏的，行文抑扬顿挫、节奏均匀，所以古人常采用口诵的方式读书，口诵时有摇头晃脑的习惯，这样可以增强节奏感，使自己更加全身心地投入其中。

【 Text 】

When learning, one should read aloud and memorize what one's leant single-mindedly. One should do so in the morning and in the evening as well.

【 Commentary 】

Ancient Chinese proses were full of rhymes and rhythms, so ancient Chinese liked to read aloud. When reading aloud, they wagged their heads to improve their sense of rhythm.

勉力勤学

Study Hard

昔仲尼	师项橐	古圣贤	尚勤学
赵中令	读鲁论	彼既仕	学且勤
披蒲编	削竹简	彼无书	且知勉
头悬梁	锥刺股	彼不教	自勤苦
如囊萤	如映雪	家虽贫	学不辍
如负薪	如挂角	身虽劳	犹苦卓
苏老泉	二十七	始发愤	读书籍
彼既老	犹悔迟	尔小生	宜早思
若梁灏	八十二	对大廷	魁多士
彼既成	众称异	尔小生	宜立志
莹八岁	能咏诗	泌七岁	能赋棋
彼颖悟	人称奇	尔幼学	当效之
蔡文姬	能辨琴	谢道韫	能咏吟
彼女子	且聪敏	尔男子	当自警
唐刘晏	方七岁	举神童	作正字
彼虽幼	身已仕	有为者	亦若是
犬守夜	鸡司晨	苟不学	曷为人
蚕吐丝	蜂酿蜜	人不学	不如物
幼而学	壮而行	上致君	下泽民
扬名声	显父母	光于前	裕于后

人遗子　金满籝　我教子　惟一经
勤有功　戏无益　戒之哉　宜勉力

　　从"昔仲尼，师项橐"到"戒之哉，宜勉力"，本部分介绍历史上勤勉好学的范例，勉励学子勤奋刻苦、孜孜不倦地读书，长大后有所作为。

　　From "Confucius learnt from the seven-year-old Xiang Tuo" to "be alert and work hard", this part introduces some good examples of diligence and encourages students to devote themselves to learning and to accomplish something when they grow up.

71. 昔仲尼　师项橐　古圣贤　尚勤学

【释文】

　　从前，孔子曾向七岁的项橐学习，他是古代的圣贤，尚且勤学好问。

【解析】

　　孔子作为一代圣人，曾向一个七岁的孩子请教，表现出孔子不耻下问的精神，孔子的这一精神被后世继承和发扬，对后世影响深远。

【 Text 】

Confucius learnt from the seven-year-old Xiang Tuo. Although he was an ancient Chinese sage, he was still studious.

【 Commentary 】

Confucius was an ancient Chinese sage, yet he learnt from a seven-year-old child, because he never felt ashamed to ask and learn from people below. The future generations are greatly influenced by such insatiable desire to learn and have inherited and developed it.

72. 赵中令　读鲁论　彼既仕　学且勤

【释文】

宋朝时的赵普，他官已经做到中书令了，仍不忘勤奋学习。

【解析】

宋太宗时的中书令赵普虽然做了大官，工作十分忙碌，但仍然没有放弃学习。赵普很爱读《论语》，一有机会就反复阅读、品味，他说过"半部《论语》治天下"的话。

【Text】

Zhao Pu of the Song Dynasty was a prime minister, yet he never forgot to learn.

【Commentary】

As prime minister of the Song Dynasty, Zhao Pu was very busy, yet he never forgot to learn. He especially loved reading *The Analects of Confucius* and said that one could rule the country by applying half of what *The Analects of Confucius* says into his ruling.

73. 披蒲编　削竹简　彼无书　且知勉

【释文】

　　西汉时，路温舒把文字抄在蒲草上阅读；公孙弘把竹子削成书简抄写《春秋》来学习。他们两人家境贫寒没有钱买书读，但仍然不忘勤奋学习。

【解析】

　　纸发明以前，所有的书都是逐字抄录在绢帛、羊皮、竹简和木牍等材料上的，因此价格十分昂贵。路温舒和公孙弘这两位古人，家里都很穷，想办法把书抄在蒲草或刻在竹子上，供自己平时苦读。

【 Text 】

　　Lu Wenshu of Western Han Dynasty copied articles on leaves of cattail and read them. Gongsun Hong of Western Han Dynasty cut bamboo into slips and wrote *The Spring and Autumn Annals* on them for learning. They both were too poor to afford books to read, but they were both very studious.

【 Commentary 】

　　Before the invention of paper, books were written on silk, sheepskin, bamboo slips, wooden tablets, etc., so they were very expensive. Lu Wenshu and Gongsun Hong were very poor, so they copied articles on leaves of cattail and self-made bamboo slips for reading.

74. 头悬梁　锥刺股　彼不教　自勤苦

【释文】

汉朝人孙敬读书时把自己的头发吊在屋梁上以防瞌睡，战国时苏秦读书瞌睡时用锥子刺大腿。他们不用别人督促而自觉勤奋苦读。

【解析】

悬梁刺股是中国古代著名的勤学苦读的范例，用以激励人发愤读书学习。除此之外，中国古代还有诸多类似的典故，比如闻鸡起舞、凿壁偷光、韦编三绝等，表现出中国自古以来的苦读传统。

[Text]

Sun Jing of Han Dynasty tied his hair on the house beam in case of feeling sleepy. Su Qin of the Warring States Period jabbed an awl into his thigh when feeling sleepy. They both devoted to learning with no need of being supervised.

[Commentary]

Tying one's hair on the house beam and jabbing one's thigh with an awl are well-known examples of tireless learning. They are told to inspire people to learn assiduously. There're some other similar stories about diligent study, such as getting up upon hearing the crow of a rooster, boring a hole on the wall to make use of the neighbor's light to study, reading books made of bamboo slips over and over again to break the leather straps that bind the bamboo slips.

75. 如囊萤　如映雪　家虽贫　学不辍

【释文】

晋朝人车胤，把萤火虫放在纱袋里用来照明读书；孙康则利用积雪的反光来照明读书。他们两人家境贫苦，却能继续求学。

【解析】

晋朝的车胤，家里贫穷，买不起油来点灯看书，于是把萤火虫装进纱布做成的袋子里，借着它们发出的微弱亮光来读书。晋朝的孙康，同样是家庭贫困，买不起油点灯读书，他不顾冬夜的寒冷，借着屋外雪地反射出的亮光读书。

【 Text 】

Che Yin of Jin Dynasty put fireflies in a gauze bag and used their light to read. Sun Kang of Jin Dynasty utilized the reflection of snow to read. They were poor, but they learnt assiduously.

【 Commentary 】

Che Yin of Jin Dynasty was too poor to afford an oil lamp, so he put fireflies in a gauze bag and used their weak light to read. Sun Kang of Jin Dynasty was too poor to afford an oil lamp, so he utilized the reflection of snow to read regardless of the coldness in the winter night.

76. 如负薪　如挂角　身虽劳　犹苦卓

【释文】

汉朝的朱买臣边担柴边读书。隋朝李密把书挂在牛角上，边放牛边读书。他们虽然身体劳累，但还是非常刻苦地学习。

【解析】

西汉朱买臣出身贫寒，靠砍柴卖钱勉强维持生计。他总是把书挂在担子前，在挑柴去卖的途中一边走路一边看书。隋朝的李密，从小帮人放牛，他就把书挂在牛角上，一边放牛一边看书。

【 Text 】

Zhu Maichen of Han Dynasty read while carrying firewood. Li Mi of Sui Dynasty hanged his books on the ox horn and read while looking after cattle on the hill. They were physically tired, yet they learnt assiduously.

【 Commentary 】

Zhu Maichen of Han Dynasty was poor and made a living by cutting firewood and selling it. He always hanged his books in front of his shoulder pole and read them on his way to selling firewood. Li Mi of Sui Dynasty looked after cattle on the hill for others when young. He hanged his books on the ox horn and read while looking after cattle.

77. 苏老泉 二十七 始发愤 读书籍
彼既老 犹悔迟 尔小生 宜早思

【释文】

宋朝的文学家苏洵，号老泉，小时候不想念书，到了二十七岁的时候，才开始下决心努力学习，后来成了大学问家。苏老泉到了老年，还后悔当初为学之迟，你们这些年轻的学子，应该及早考虑用功读书。

【解析】

宋代著名文学家苏洵和他两个儿子苏轼与苏辙，是中国文学史上十分有名的人物，他们的学问都很高，文章也都写得很好，被后人合称为"三苏"。

【 Text 】

Su Xun of Song Dynasty, whose pseudonym was Laoquan, did not like reading when young. He made his decision to devote to learning at 27 and became a great scholar. When old, Su Xun regretted not learning at an earlier age. Young as you are, you should devote yourselves to learning.

【 Commentary 】

Su Xun, the great writer in the Song Dynasty, together with his two sons Su Shi and Su Zhe, was well-known in the history of Chinese literature. They were well learned and great writers. They were called Three Sus by later generations.

78. 若梁灏　八十二　对大廷　魁多士
彼既成　众称异　尔小生　宜立志

【释文】

　　宋朝有个梁灏，八十二岁时才考中状元，在金殿上对皇帝提出的问题对答如流，其他士子都不如他。梁灏这么大年纪，尚能获得成功，不能不使大家感到惊异。你们这些年轻学子，应该立定志向及早用功。

【解析】

　　梁灏，宋代人，最好读书。他生于五代，从后晋天福三年开始应试，经历后汉、后周，不中状元，誓不甘心。到了八十二岁，宋太宗雍熙二年，才状元及第。金殿对策，独占鳌头。这段话强调了少年立志的重要性。

【 Text 】

Liang Hao of Song Dynasty came first in the highest imperial examination and was honored with Number One Scholar at 82. He could answer up to every question posed by the emperor at the royal palace, outperforming other scholars. People felt amazed that Liang Hao could achieve success at such an old age. Young as you are, you should devote yourselves to learning.

【 Commentary 】

Liang Hao of Song Dynasty was an avid learner. Born at the Five Dynasties period, he started to sit for the imperial examination at the third Tianfu year of Later Jin and continued to take the examination year after year in the succeeding Later Han and Later Zhou, but he did not come first in the highest imperial examination until the second Yongxi year of the reign of Emperor Taizong of Song when he was 82. He could answer up to every question posed by the emperor at the royal palace, outperforming other scholars. This passage stresses the importance of devoting to learning at an early age.

79. 莹八岁　能咏诗　泌七岁　能赋棋
##　　彼颖悟　人称奇　尔幼学　当效之

【释文】

　　北魏有个叫祖莹的人，八岁就能吟诗。唐朝有个叫李泌的人，七岁时就能以下棋为题而作出诗赋。他们两个人的聪明和才智，在当时很受人们的称赞，众人认为这是一件了不起的奇事。你们这些年幼的学生，应当效法他们。

【解析】

　　北魏的祖莹，字元珍，从小好读书，日夜勤读，时人称他为小圣童，八岁就能咏诗成章，后为秘书监著作郎。唐朝李泌，七岁能作棋赋，后历任四朝宰相，为社稷重臣。

【 Text 】

Zu Ying of Northern Wei was able to recite poems at the age of eight and Li Mi of Tang Dynasty was able to write poems with the theme of playing Chinese chess. They were highly commended by others for their intelligence and people felt amazed at their talents. Young as you are, you should emulate them.

【 Commentary 】

Zu Ying of Northern Wei (courtesy name was Yuan Zhen) was an avid learner and was called a child prodigy. Zu Ying was able to recite poems at the age of eight and he became a high-ranking official when he grew up. Li Mi of Tang Dynasty was able to write poems with the theme of playing Chinese chess at the age of seven and became Prime Minister for four emperors when he grew up.

80. 蔡文姬　能辨琴　谢道韫　能咏吟
　　彼女子　且聪敏　尔男子　当自警

【释文】

　　东汉末年的蔡文姬能分辨琴声好坏，东晋才女谢道韫则能出口成诗。蔡文姬和谢道韫两个女孩子，既聪明又敏捷；你们这些男孩子应当自我警惕，好好努力。

【解析】

　　蔡文姬是东汉学者蔡邕的女儿。她天资过人，尤其在音乐方面非常有天赋，她能准确分辨琴声好坏，甚至能听出弹奏者的感情。谢道韫是东晋宰相谢安的侄女。她才思敏捷，很小的时候就会吟诗作对，所作的咏雪诗句甚至压倒了其他兄弟。

【 Text 】

    Cai Wenji who lived at the end of Eastern Han Dynasty could distinguish the sound quality of Qin, a traditional Chinese musical instrument. Xie Daoyun, a talented girl living in Eastern Jin could make impromptu poems. Both Cai Wenji and Xie Daoyun were girls, yet they were smart. Boys like you should study hard.

【 Commentary 】

    Cai Wenji was the daughter of Cai Yong, a scholar of Eastern Han. She was talented. She had a gift for music and could distinguish the sound quality of Qin, a traditional Chinese musical instrument and have insight into the emotions of the player of Qin. Xie Daoyun was the niece of the Prime Minister Xie An of Eastern Jin. She was smart and could make poems at a young age and her poems were better than that of her brothers.

81. 唐刘晏　方七岁　举神童　作正字
彼虽幼　身已仕　有为者　亦若是

【释文】

　　唐朝的刘晏，七岁时，就被推举为神童，并且做了负责刊正文字的官。刘晏虽然年纪小，但已经做官。有作为的人，应当像这样。

【解析】

　　唐朝的刘晏，聪明好学，小小年纪就能作诗写文章。唐玄宗听说了他的事迹，为了表示赞赏与鼓励，选拔他担任正字官，负责校对书籍文字。

【 Text 】

Liu Yan of Tang Dynasty was generally considered as a child prodigy and was promoted to an official in charge of text proof reading at seven. Young as he was, he was promoted to an official. You should emulate him if you want to accomplish something.

【 Commentary 】

Liu Yan of Tang Dynasty was smart and assiduous in learning. He was able to write poems and articles at a young age. When knowing his story, Emperor Xuanzong promoted him to an official in charge of text proof reading as a reward.

82. 犬守夜　鸡司晨　苟不学　曷为人

【释文】

狗在夜间会替人看守家门，鸡在每天早晨天亮时报晓。人如果不能用心学习有用的本领，还怎么做人呢？

【解析】

此处以狗能看门、鸡会报晓来说明人应当学习、掌握立身处世的本领。一犬一鸡，尚有可取之处，作为万物之灵的人，更应当不断学习、不断进步。

[Text]

Dogs watch the door for their owners. Roosters crow at dawn. How can one establish oneself in the world if one does not devote to learning?

[Commentary]

The passage stresses the importance of learning and acquiring skills for one to establish oneself in the world by using the analogy of watchdogs and crowing roosters. A dog and a rooster have their strengths, so mankind, as the wisest of all creatures should keep leaning and making progress.

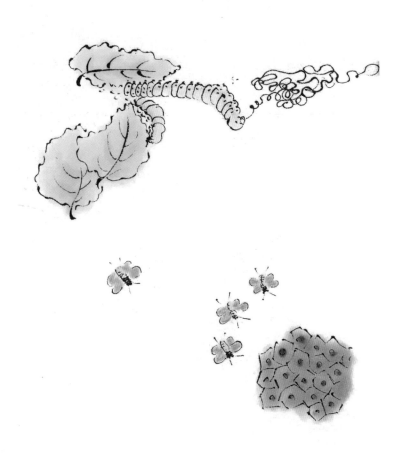

83. 蚕吐丝　蜂酿蜜　人不学　不如物

【释文】

　　蚕吐丝以供人们做衣料，蜜蜂可以采花酿蜜，供人们食用。而人要是不懂得学习，没有为社会服务的本领，就真不如动物了。

【解析】

　　蚕、蜂都是小小昆虫，但对人类的贡献巨大。蚕儿和蜜蜂尚且如此，人们更应该知道积极进取，志存高远。

【 Text 】

Silkworms spin silk, which is used as the material for clothing. Bees make honey, which is used as food. If mankind does not learn and acquire skills, he is not the equal of animals.

【 Commentary 】

Silkworms and bees are small insects, yet they make outstanding contributions to mankind. So mankind should be enterprising and aim high.

84. 幼而学 壮而行 上致君 下泽民

【释文】

我们要在幼年时努力学习，长大后有所作为，对上报效国家，对下造福百姓。

【解析】

人在少年时期，是最有朝气的，接受知识的能力和记忆力也是很强的，应趁着年幼时期的大好光阴努力学习，掌握知识和本领。读书应注意学以致用，这样才能够把学到的知识贡献出来。

【 Text 】

We should study hard when young and serve our country and benefit the people when grow up.

【 Commentary 】

Men are full of vitality and they are quick learners with a good memory when young, so men should devote themselves to learning when young and acquire knowledge and skills. Men should put into practice what they have learnt.

85. 扬名声　显父母　光于前　裕于后

【释文】

　　使自己的名声远扬，让父母感到荣耀，给祖先带来光彩，为后代留下财富。

【解析】

　　"十年寒窗无人问，一举成名天下知。"如果能够为报效国家、造福民众贡献自己的知识和力量，那么，不仅自己很光荣，为父母、祖先争得荣誉，还能在精神、物质上给子孙后代以帮助。

【Text】

One should make a name for himself and bring honor to his parents and his ancestors and leave a fortune for his offspring.

【Commentary】

After many years' hard study noticed by none, he will have his fame spread far and wide when winning his honors. If one serves his country and benefits common people with his knowledge and skills, one will not only make a name, but also bring honor to his parents and his ancestors and leave material and moral wealth for his offspring.

86. 人遗子　金满籝　我教子　惟一经

【释文】

　　有的人遗留给子孙后代的是装满竹箱的金银钱财，而我教育子孙的，只有一本经书。

【解析】

　　知识是人类宝贵的财富。金银财宝再多，对于坐吃山空的人来说，也有花光用尽的时候。但如果通晓了儒家经典，明白了做人处世的道理，也就掌握了安身立命的根本。

[Text]

Some leave piles of gold and silver and other material wealth for their offspring while I leave Confucian classics for them.

[Commentary]

Knowledge is the precious wealth to mankind. An idler will eat away his whole fortune. Nonetheless, if one is well-versed in Confucian classics, one will know how to behave oneself which is the basis for one to establish himself in the world.

87. 勤有功　戏无益　戒之哉　宜勉力

【释文】

　　只有勤奋才会有好的收获，而只顾贪玩则没有什么好处。一定要警醒啊，应当好好努力。

【解析】

　　年轻人要时刻提醒自己，珍惜大好的时光，持之以恒地读书学习，才能获得成功；相反，如果一味地贪玩嬉戏，是没有什么好处的。

【 Text 】

One will achieve success through hard work while larking about will yield no good results, so be alert and work hard.

【 Commentary 】

Young people should constantly remind themselves of cherishing the precious time by devoting themselves to study. Only by doing so, they will attain success. On the contrary, if they enjoy playing endlessly, they will accomplish nothing.